Illustrator:
Howard Chaney

Editor:
Stephanie Buehler, MP.W., M.A.

Editorial Project Manager:
Karen J. Goldfluss, M.S. Ed.

Editor in Chief:
Sharon Coan, M.S. Ed.

Art Director:
Elayne Roberts

Associate Designer:
Denise Bauer

Cover Artist:
Marc Kaslauskas

Product Manager:
Phil Garcia

Imaging:
Ralph Olmedo, Jr.

Publishers:
Rachelle Cracchiolo, M.S. Ed.
Mary Dupuy Smith, M.S. Ed.

primary

Author:

Julia Jasmine, M.A.

Teacher Created Materials, Inc.
P.O. Box 1040
Huntington Beach, CA 92647
ISBN-1-57690-062-2

©*1997 Teacher Created Materials, Inc.*   Made in U.S.A.

Table of Contents

Introduction

Use *Instant Social Studies* to enhance your social studies program and give your students something fun to do and think about every single day. This book contains calendar-related lessons for every week of the year. Each lesson includes five activities—a week of instant social studies! As an extra bonus each lesson contains a language arts component to supplement your regular curriculum.

Instant Social Studies can be used in two ways: by date (the lessons are in chronological order) or by subject (consult the index).

Instant Social Studies will respond to several needs of teachers. It will provide fresh material for experienced teachers and materials for the entire calendar year—a necessity in the increasingly popular year-round school and one that is not addressed by traditional curriculum resources.

Background

The first day of the new year has always been considered a new beginning, a time to start over. In the United States, New Year's Eve and New Year's Day are celebrated on December 31 and January 1 of each year because of our calendar. People in other parts of the world, or people in the United States who use different calendars, celebrate the new year at different times.

Making It Work

Concentrate your recognition of the new year on a little of its history and on some of the costumes associated with its celebration. After the parties are over, people in the United States often make New Year's resolutions. Resolutions can be thought of as personal plans or promises a person makes.

The new year is celebrated in different ways, depending on the culture. In Asia, people celebrate the lunar new year. They clean their houses, pay their bills, and have great feasts. In China, people call the new year "Sun Nin." In Vietnam, it is called "Tet." In Iran, the New Year is called "Noruz" and is celebrated in March. Noruz lasts for two weeks and ends with a picnic.

Day 1—Janus

Materials

- drawing paper (8 ½" x 11"/22 cm x 28 cm) and art materials
- silhouette of a profile (Enlarge, copy, and cut out one of the drawings below.)

Activity

Tell students about Janus who was the ancient Roman god of doorways and of beginnings and endings. Janus had two faces so he could look both ways, back into the old year and forward into the new one. Our month of January was named after him.

Have students fold their paper in half to make a greeting card. Give them the silhouette of a profile and have them trace it on the front of the card so it looks both ways. Students can color and decorate their cards and write "Happy New Year" under the picture. Their own message (to their parents, perhaps) can be written on the inside of the card.

Day 2—Sun Nin

Materials

- paper towels
- trash bags
- non-toxic cleaning spray
- small banners (enlarge and copy design below)

Activity

Tell students about the Chinese custom of making everything sparkling clean for the new year. Organize teams to wipe off desks and countertops; straighten book shelves and locate separated sets of books; and find misplaced pieces of puzzles, games, and sets of manipulatives, putting them where they belong. When the clean up is finished, give everyone a small banner with the symbols for Happy New Year ("Gung hoy fat choy") in Chinese. Have students color the symbols black and the background red.

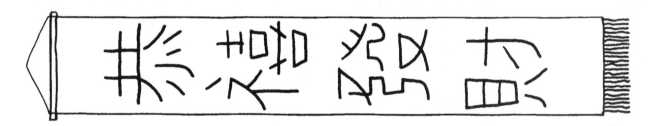

Day 3—Tet

Materials

- pencils and paper
- red construction paper, cut in half horizontally
- ballpoint pens or fine-line markers in black
- a book of children's poetry (*A Child's Garden of Verses* by Robert Louis Stevenson, for example)

Activity

The celebration of Tet, the Vietnamese New Year, centers around the family. One popular activity is writing poems about one's family.

Read some simple rhyming verses to your students. *A Child's Garden of Verses* by Robert Louis Stevenson is always a nice choice. (This activity stresses rhyming verse as rhyming words give students a chance to practice phonics skills.)

Write a few family-oriented words on the board and brainstorm rhyming words for each of them to give students a head start. Try these: mom, dad, love, safe, happy, warm, and so on.

Have students write their poems on regular paper and edit them before copying them on the strips of red paper for display on the bulletin board.

Day 4—Noruz

Materials

- shallow bowl
- quick-sprouting seeds (lentils or grains of wheat are used in the Middle East)
- chart for recording observations

Activity

Noruz (or "Now Ruz") literally means "new day." It is the Middle Eastern New Year. It begins on March 21, the beginning of spring, but lasts two weeks and ends with an outdoor picnic. Seeds are sprinkled in water so that their sprouts can represent the new life that comes with spring.

Point out the Middle East on your classroom map of the world. Note the names of the various countries in this area.

Talk about spring as a kind of beginning.

Sprinkle some seeds in a shallow bowl of water.

Watch the seeds from day to day and record what you see on a chart.

Day 5—Resolutions

Materials

- pencils and paper

Activity

Discuss resolutions. Students can think of these as promises they make to themselves or as plans for the future. Ask each student to think of at least one resolution.

Depending on the age group, students can dictate their resolutions, write them briefly, or elaborate at great length. They can copy and illustrate their resolutions for public display on the bulletin board, write them in a journal, or store them in their portfolios for future reference.

You can help students with their resolutions by distributing paper and asking them to start with the following statement:

> ## This year I plan to . . .

Background

Betsy Ross was born on January 1, 1752. She is credited with making what became the first flag of the United States. The flag she sewed together by hand in 1776 was adopted by the Continental Congress on June 14, 1777. Betsy Ross's original flag had 13 alternating red and white stripes and 13 white stars on a blue field. After a few changes in design when new states were added (at one point, there were 15 stars and 15 stripes), a law was passed in 1818 specifying that there would be 13 stripes to represent the 13 original colonies. A new star would be added to the blue field for each new state.

Making It Work

Give your students as much background about Betsy Ross as you think they will be interested in. Use your classroom flag to demonstrate what you are describing when you point out the colors and the stars and stripes.

Day 1—Flag Facts

Materials

- classroom flag
- wall map of the United States

Activity

This activity is designed to be an oral exercise to establish a general base of information. See what the students already know and tell them the answers they don't know. Go back and repeat some of the questions and answers for reinforcement.

Where did Betsy Ross live? Find it on the map. (Philadelphia, Pennsylvania)

Why did she sew the flag by hand? (no sewing machines)

Why are the red stripes on the outside edges? (so it can be seen against the sky)

What are some other names for the flag? (Old Glory; the Star Spangled Banner; the Red, White, and Blue)

How many stars did Betsy Ross's flag have? (thirteen)

How many stars does the flag have now? Why? (50 stars, 50 states)

How many stripes did Betsy Ross's flag have? Why? (13 stripes, 13 colonies)

How many stripes does the flag have now? Why? (13 stripes, adding more would have made it an odd design or shape)

Which were the last two states to join the United States? Find them on the map. (Alaska, 49th, in 1959; Hawaii, 50th, in 1959)

What were the names of the 13 original colonies (states)? Find them on the map. (Connecticut, Delaware, Georgia, Maryland, Massachusetts, New Hampshire, New Jersey, New York, North Carolina, Pennsylvania, Rhode Island, South Carolina, and Virginia)

Day 2—Draw the Flag

Materials

- 8 ½" x 11" (22 cm x 28 cm) white paper (or enlarge copies of flag below)
- pencils and rulers
- crayons
- self-stick white stars

Activity

Depending on the age of your students, have them draw their own flags or simply color an enlargement of the flag below. If students are going to draw their own flags, show them how to measure the paper and divide it into thirteen equal stripes. (Each stripe should be a little wider than ⁵/₈"/1.6 cm.) They can look at the classroom flag to estimate how far over and down the blue field should come. This is a very satisfying exercise for some students, but it is a tricky assignment and may be too frustrating for others. Have copies of the flag below available for those students to use.

Day 3—Songs About Flags

Materials

- recording of songs about the flag such as "The Star Spangled Banner," "Three Cheers for the Red, White, and Blue," "You're a Grand Old Flag"

Activity

Play some of the patriotic tunes for your students. Have students vote for their favorite(s) and begin to learn the lyrics. You can do this as part of your daily opening ritual or in preparation for an upcoming patriotic program.

Day 4—Design Your Own Flag

Materials

- art supplies
- books with information about flags, particularly the meanings of symbols and colors

Activity

Tell students a little about the meanings of the symbols contained in the U.S. flag. Older students can do their own research if you wish. (White stands for purity, red for courage, and blue for loyalty; stars symbolize hope.)

Have students design their own personal flags, choosing colors and symbols that are meaningful to them. Ask them to be ready to explain their designs.

Day 5—The Pledge of Allegiance

Materials

- words to the Pledge of Allegiance printed on a large poster board
- copy of pledge, below, printed on the other side of the poster board

Activity

Help students to define and understand the words of the pledge:

I pledge (promise) allegiance (to be loyal) to the flag (symbol) of the United States of America (one country made up of 50 states) and to the republic (kind of government in which people vote for the ones who make laws) for which it stands (that it represents)—one nation (country), under God (the Creator), with liberty (freedom) and justice (fair laws) for all.

Occasionally, after saying the pledge, ask who remembers what "pledge" means, "allegiance," and so on. Review definitions as you wish.

Background

On January 11, 1868, a dairy distributing milk in Brooklyn, New York delivered the product to customers in glass bottles, marking the first time this had ever been done.

Making It Work

Ask how many of your students have ever had their milk delivered by a milkman. Where do they get their milk? What kind of container does it come in?

Day 1—Milk Around the World

Materials

- classroom wall map of the world
- encyclopedias or other illustrated reference materials

Activity

Give students these interesting facts about the history of milk in an oral, large-group lesson. Find each area on the world map. Find pictures of these animals and the countries where they live in reference materials.

- Records from ancient Egypt, Mesopotamia (now Iran), and India show that people raised dairy cattle at least 6,000 years ago.
- Cows provide much of the milk used in the United States.
- Goat milk is popular in countries around the Mediterranean Sea, Norway, Switzerland, Latin America, parts of Asia and Africa, and in the mountain areas of the southwestern U.S.
- Camel milk is used in the deserts of Arabia and Central Asia.
- Llama milk is used in the Andes regions of South America.
- People get milk from reindeer, horses, and yaks in some Arctic regions.
- Sheep provide milk in Spain, Italy, and the Netherlands.
- Water buffalo supply milk in the rain forests of India and the Philippines and in much of Southeast Asia.

Day 2—History of the Dairy Industry

Materials

- classroom wall map of the world
- encyclopedias or other illustrated reference materials
- copies of the activity below (or statements written on the board)

Activity

Name _____   Date _____

Use reference materials to find the answers to these questions.

1. Modern dairy cows are descended from wild cattle that roamed the forests of _____.

2. Dairy cows were brought to the Jamestown colony in Virginia in _____.

3. The chief source of milk for hundreds of years was _____.

4. Families used the milk they needed and the rest they _____.

5. As cities began to grow, what law about cows was passed? _____.

6. What did farmers do then? _____.

7. People did not know much about germs in those days, and milk was often not safe to drink until Louis Pasteur discovered a way to_____.

- -

Answers

1. northeastern Europe
2. 1611
3. the family cow
4. sold or traded to neighbors
5. Cows could not be kept within the city limits.
6. Farmers increased the sizes of their herds and started dairies.
7. kill germs in fluids with heat (pasteurization)

Day 3—The Milk Makers

Materials

- *The Milk Makers* by Gail Gibbons (Macmillan, 1985)

Activity

The Milk Makers is a brief book that tells how cows make milk, how the milk is processed, and how many products are made from it. Read this book aloud to your class, discussing the information and illustrations as you go along. Leave the book (several copies, if possible) in your classroom library for students to explore on their own.

Day 4—Kinds of Cows

Materials

- encyclopedias or other illustrated reference materials
- simple line drawings of cows duplicated (coloring books are a good source)

Activity

Have students find information in reference books about the three most important kinds of dairy cows (Holstein, Jersey, and Guernsey) and color and label their line drawings.

Day 5—Ice Cream Experience

Materials

- an ice cream churn and necessary ingredients for making ice cream

  or

  store-bought ice cream
- paper plates, cups, or bowls, plastic spoons, napkins

Activity

Finish off your dairy week with an ice cream party. If possible, make fresh ice cream in the classroom. This is a great experience that not many children get to have. Ice cream from the store, however, is also a great experience.

Background

A. A. (Alan Alexander) Milne was born on January 18, 1882, in London, England. He wrote four books for children: *When We Were Very Young*, *Now We Are Six*, *Winnie-the-Pooh*, and *The House at Pooh Corner*. These books, illustrated by Ernest Shepard and published by E. P. Dutton between 1924 and 1928, have become some of the most popular books ever written for children. They are available in many editions and have become the basis for an extensive series of animated Disney movies. The first four animated stories are classic stories thats follow the texts of the books very closely.

Making It Work

Plan to show one or two videos of the classic Pooh stories. If you do not have these in your classroom collection, your students will probably be glad to bring some from home. The titles you will want to choose from are "*Winnie-the-Pooh and a Day for Eeyore*," "*Winnie-the-Pooh and The Honey Tree*," "*Winnie-the-Pooh and Tigger Too*," and "*Winnie-the-Pooh and the Blustery Day*" (an Academy Award winner).

Have on hand some of the regular, hardcover editions of the Pooh books. These are of special interest because in many cases the pages are used as backgrounds in the animated stories. For example, in one video Tigger walks down the edges of the printed words. Your students will enjoy finding these original pages and comparing them with the video images.

Day 1—Role Playing

Materials

- TV and VCR
- one or more classic Winnie-the-Pooh videos

Activity

Show at least one video to your class. After reviewing the video, ask students to do silent role-playing. Call on volunteers for these characters. Some suggestions follow, but children will, of course, have their own ideas. Ask them to "be" the characters.

Pooh: dip hand into jar of honey and pretend to eat

Piglet: look shy, twist feet and hands, look down, act "little"

Rabbit: act bossy, look worried

Tigger: bouncy, cheerful

Kanga: sweet, motherly

Roo: bouncy on a small scale

Eeyore: depressed, sad

Day 1—Role Playing *(cont.)*

After each role-playing experience, ask these questions:

Who was_____pretending to be?

How do you know?

What did_____do that told you?

Encourage the group to discuss the role playing. How did it feel to be the character? How did it feel to watch? Was it hard or easy? Would they like to do it again?

Invite students to bring in any stuffed Pooh characters they have at home to use on Day 4.

Day 2—Map Study

Materials

- world map
- copies of outline map of England (enlarge map below)
- pencils and colored pencils
- selection of books containing pictures of the English countryside as well as the larger cities

Activity

Point out England to students on the world map. Discuss its location in relation to the United States and to other countries in the world. Ask students to give their ideas about how the Pooh stories became so popular in the United States, considering the distance between the U.S. and England. (Even though the United States is separated from England by the Atlantic Ocean, the two countries have a great deal in common, including history and language.)

Have students refer to the world map to mark some important cities on their outline maps of England.

Day 3—Character Descriptions

Materials

- writing and drawing materials

Activity

Write the names of the Pooh characters on the board. Remind them of the role-playing experiences they had on Day 1 and then have students brainstorm words that describe their character traits.

Have each student draw a picture of his or her favorite character and either dictate or write a description of that character at the bottom of the picture. Display work on the bulletin board.

Day 4—Stuffed Animal Theater

Materials

- classroom puppet theater (or a cleared-off table with a sheet over it)
- visiting stuffed animals (clearly tagged with their owners' names)

Activity

Divide the class into groups. Have each group prepare and present a short "puppet show" using stuffed animals from home. Enjoy and appreciate!

Day 5—Pooh Party for A. A. Milne

Materials

- a birthday cake or cookies
- milk or juice
- napkins and cups

Activity

Sing "Happy Birthday" to A. A. Milne. If you have rhythm instruments in the classroom, have an impromptu birthday parade. Have students tell about their favorite parts of the stories. Read aloud a chapter or poem from one of the books if time allows.

Figure out A. A. Milne's age and then the age of the Pooh books based on today's date.

Background

Australia was first settled by colonists on January 26, 1788. It is an island continent that drifted away from the rest of Earth's landmass so long ago that its animals are different from those in any other part of the world. Many of the animals are marsupials, animals that carry their young in pouches.

Making It Work

Obtain a movie or video that shows the different climates and regions of Australia in order to give your students a visual context for the animals they will be learning about. Have books and other illustrated materials available in your classroom, such as posters and travel brochures about Australian destinations.

Enlarge the form below and make four copies. Cut out the pictures of the Australian animals on page 16 and tape one picture to each form. Then copy sets of each of these pages for your class to use as they write an illustrated book about the animals.

Name _____   Date _____

_____

_____

_____

_____

Animal

_____

_____

_____

_____

Making It Work *(cont.)*

Day 1—Kangaroo

Materials
- kangaroo (See page 16.)
- pencil and crayons

Activity
Depending on the age of your group, have students research and write a report or create a story about kangaroos. (Small children can dictate stories.)

Day 2—Koala

Materials
- koala (See page 16.)
- pencil and crayons

Activity
Depending on the age of your group, have students research and write a report or create a story about koalas. (Small children can dictate stories.)

Day 3—Platypus

Materials
- platypus (See page 16.)
- pencil and crayons

Activity
Depending on the age of your group, have students research and write a report or create a story about the platypus. (Small children can dictate stories.)

Day 4—Emu

Materials
- emu (See page 16.)
- pencil and crayons

Activity
Depending on the age of your group, have students research and write a report or create a story about the emu. (Small children can dictate stories.)

Day 5—Cover

Materials
- construction paper
- pencil and crayons
- completed Australian animal pages

Activity
Have children fold construction paper in half to make folders for their completed stories or reports. They can decorate the cover and write "Australian Animals" on the front. Insert the four pages and staple.

Background

February 2 is Groundhog Day. Legend has it that the groundhog, or woodchuck, ends its hibernation and comes out of its hole on that day. If the weather is sunny and the groundhog sees its shadow, winter will last for six more weeks. If the weather is overcast and it doesn't see its shadow, winter will be short. This event gets great media coverage, especially in Punxsutawney, Pennsylvania, where a famous groundhog, Phil, lives.

Making It Work

Encourage students to look for coverage of Groundhog Day in the newspaper and on television news. Focus some discussion on other hibernating animals. Among the many mammals that hibernate are bears, chipmunks, squirrels, and bats. In addition, some reptiles hibernate, as do many insects. Another interesting subject for discussion is folklore about weather prediction, i.e., a ring of light around the moon predicts rain for the following day.

Day 1—Media Coverage

Materials

- copies of the form for reporting on media coverage (below)

Activity

Give students the form below and ask them to use it on Groundhog Day. They can report their results to the class, bringing in newspaper clippings and so on.

Name _____   Date _____

Groundhog Day

I found my information_____.

The groundhog was seen at_____

in _____.

The groundhog's name is _____.

Other information:_____

_____

Day 2—Hibernation

Materials

- encyclopedias or other illustrated reference materials
- writing materials

Activity

Have students research and write a brief explanation of hibernation—what it is, which animals hibernate, how the animals know when to go to sleep and when to wake up, and so on.

Ask volunteers to read their work aloud to the class. Pool the information gathered by the class and make a "Hibernation Facts" chart that includes information about . . .

. . . animals that hibernate.

. . . what the animals do before hibernating.

. . . what the animals do when they wake up.

Day 3—The Groundhog Story

Materials

- writing materials

Activity

Have students pretend that they are the groundhog who has just stuck its head out of its hole. What does it see? How does it feel? Does it like having all those cameras pointed at it? What will it do next? Ask students to tell a story from the point of view of one particular groundhog. Have them be sure to tell where it lives and what its name is.

Have a read-around of the completed stories. Give students time to revise and edit. Then have them copy their stories on good paper and post them on a creative writing bulletin board in your classroom.

Day 4—What's the Weather Like Today?

Materials

- weather pages from a daily newspaper (at least one for every pair of students)
- classroom wall maps of the United States and the world

Activity

As a large group, look over the weather page, reading and discussing some of the information: local highs and lows, highs and lows for cities in the United States, and highs and lows for cities around the world that are of interest to your students.

Look at the predicted highs and lows, too. Discuss how these are predicted. Without getting too technical, point out the weather map that shows the symbols used by meteorologists.

Day 5—Keeping a Winter Weather Chart

Materials

- calendar pages for February and March with large squares in which to write

Activity

Track the weather for six weeks, beginning with February 2, Groundhog Day, recording the daily highs and lows and a description of the weather.

At the end of six weeks, have a class discussion of the groundhog as a weather predictor:

- What did the groundhog predict?
- What really happened?
- Was the groundhog right or wrong?

Background

Although Valentine's Day is celebrated in many parts of the world on February 14, no one really knows how it started. It may have been named after a man named Valentine who was a priest in Rome around 300 A.D. He was put to death for being a Christian and later recognized as a saint. However it began, Valentine's Day was a popular celebration during the Middle Ages, when people recited or sang their greetings in ballads because few people could read or write.

Making It Work

- Talk about life in the Middle Ages. Show students pictures of lords and ladies dressed in medieval costumes. Start to gather scarves and pieces of material to drape into costumes.

Day 1—Life in the Middle Ages

Materials

- encyclopedias or other illustrated reference materials

Activity

Have a whole-class oral lesson about the Middle Ages. Talk about the clothes worn by the wealthy and how we don't know much about what common people wore. (Most encyclopedias have pages of colored illustrations of the clothes worn by the nobility in different periods.) Talk about what life must have been like when hardly anyone could read or write. (There were no newspapers, magazines, books, letters, cards, and so on. Only the very richest people went to any kind of school.)

Tell the students that people celebrated Valentine's Day during the Middle Ages. Ask questions such as the following:

- If the person you wanted to give a valentine to couldn't read, what could you do?

- If you couldn't write, how could you give a valentine to someone?

- What do you suppose the people in the Middle Ages did to express their love in a special way? (Either elicit the response that people must have spoken or sung their valentine greetings or give students that information.)

Suggest that your classroom have a Middle Ages Valentine's Day celebration, ending with a party for parents or other relatives or friends (see pages 22 and 23).

Background

The first telephone book was distributed on February 21, 1878, in New Haven, Connecticut, which is also the location of the first telephone exchange. There were fifty listings in the book.

Making It Work

Encourage students to discuss telephone usage in their own families. Do they have more than one phone? More than one phone number? Do their parents have pagers or cellular phones? Can they imagine life without the telephone? How did people communicate or keep track of one another before telephones existed?

Day 1—The History of the Telephone

Materials

- encyclopedias or other illustrated reference materials

Activity

Have a whole-class oral discussion about the history of the telephone. Use the introductory facts below to get students started. Volunteers can use your reference books to find out more about each topic as you go along.

- The telephone was invented by Alexander Graham Bell.

- The invention of the telephone was almost by accident. Bell was in the process of working on another invention.

- Bell had an assistant named Thomas Watson. They had a famous conversation.

- The first two-way, long-distance conversation was between Boston and Cambridge, Massachusetts, a distance of two miles.

- The first telephone switchboard went into operation in 1878. Until then, each phone had to be connected to all the others.

- Many people claimed to have invented the telephone, but in 1888 the Supreme Court of the United States upheld Bell's patents.

- Bell and Watson, along with two other men who had backed Bell's experiments, formed the Bell Telephone Company in 1878.

- Early phone service was accomplished through operators who said, "Number, please," when the person placing the call picked up the phone. The caller gave the operator the number, and she (almost all operators were women) made the connection.

- Later, phones had rotary dials for dialing the number being called. Still later, dials were replaced by buttons.

Background

The first telephone book was distributed on February 21, 1878, in New Haven, Connecticut, which is also the location of the first telephone exchange. There were fifty listings in the book.

Making It Work

Encourage students to discuss telephone usage in their own families. Do they have more than one phone? More than one phone number? Do their parents have pagers or cellular phones? Can they imagine life without the telephone? How did people communicate or keep track of one another before telephones existed?

Day 1—The History of the Telephone

Materials

- encyclopedias or other illustrated reference materials

Activity

Have a whole-class oral discussion about the history of the telephone. Use the introductory facts below to get students started. Volunteers can use your reference books to find out more about each topic as you go along.

- The telephone was invented by Alexander Graham Bell.

- The invention of the telephone was almost by accident. Bell was in the process of working on another invention.

- Bell had an assistant named Thomas Watson. They had a famous conversation.

- The first two-way, long-distance conversation was between Boston and Cambridge, Massachusetts, a distance of two miles.

- The first telephone switchboard went into operation in 1878. Until then, each phone had to be connected to all the others.

- Many people claimed to have invented the telephone, but in 1888 the Supreme Court of the United States upheld Bell's patents.

- Bell and Watson, along with two other men who had backed Bell's experiments, formed the Bell Telephone Company in 1878.

- Early phone service was accomplished through operators who said, "Number, please," when the person placing the call picked up the phone. The caller gave the operator the number, and she (almost all operators were women) made the connection.

- Later, phones had rotary dials for dialing the number being called. Still later, dials were replaced by buttons.

Day 3—Making Costumes (cont.)

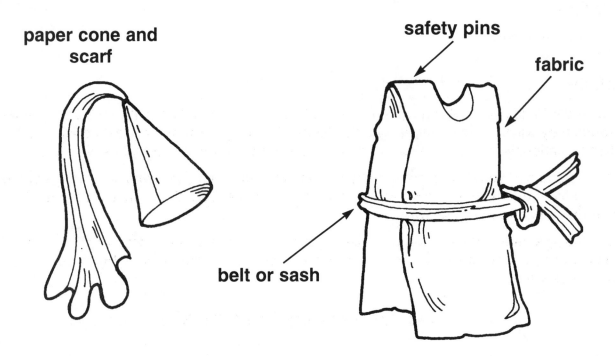

paper cone and scarf

safety pins

fabric

belt or sash

Day 4—Rehearsal

Materials

- costumes

Activity

Have a dress rehearsal. Set up a chair or chairs and have students present their valentines to imaginary "honored guests."

Day 5—Middle Ages Valentine's Day Party

Materials

- party supplies
- cookies and punch (or whatever you decide to serve)

Activity

Combine your party with the performance of the oral valentines. If any of your students are without an honored guest, encourage them to invite a favorite teacher or other adult at school.

Day 2—Creating a Poem or Song

Materials

- none necessary

Activity

Have students decide on the people they wish to invite to the party and begin creating verses or songs they will present to those people. Remind them to invite their guests orally—no written invitations! (For "insurance," send discrete party invitations home in envelopes!)

Help students decide whether or not they will need to write out these verses or songs in order to memorize them. Remind them that people in the Middle Ages didn't have a choice—they had to memorize their valentines!

Have students take several "memory breaks" each day to practice the song or poem until it comes time to actually invite people to the party. Allow them time to share how their experiences went.

Day 3—Making Costumes

Materials

- an assortment of scarves and lengths of fabric
- belts, sashes, and ribbon
- clothes from a dress-up box, if you have one
- construction paper, scissors, tape, etc.
- a full-length mirror, if possible

Activity

Have students create their costumes for the Middle Ages party. See ideas below and on the next page.

Background

Although Valentine's Day is celebrated in many parts of the world on February 14, no one really knows how it started. It may have been named after a man named Valentine who was a priest in Rome around 300 A.D. He was put to death for being a Christian and later recognized as a saint. However it began, Valentine's Day was a popular celebration during the Middle Ages, when people recited or sang their greetings in ballads because few people could read or write.

Making It Work

- Talk about life in the Middle Ages. Show students pictures of lords and ladies dressed in medieval costumes. Start to gather scarves and pieces of material to drape into costumes.

Day 1—Life in the Middle Ages

Materials

- encyclopedias or other illustrated reference materials

Activity

Have a whole-class oral lesson about the Middle Ages. Talk about the clothes worn by the wealthy and how we don't know much about what common people wore. (Most encyclopedias have pages of colored illustrations of the clothes worn by the nobility in different periods.) Talk about what life must have been like when hardly anyone could read or write. (There were no newspapers, magazines, books, letters, cards, and so on. Only the very richest people went to any kind of school.)

Tell the students that people celebrated Valentine's Day during the Middle Ages. Ask questions such as the following:

- If the person you wanted to give a valentine to couldn't read, what could you do?

- If you couldn't write, how could you give a valentine to someone?

- What do you suppose the people in the Middle Ages did to express their love in a special way? (Either elicit the response that people must have spoken or sung their valentine greetings or give students that information.)

Suggest that your classroom have a Middle Ages Valentine's Day celebration, ending with a party for parents or other relatives or friends (see pages 22 and 23).

Day 2—Exploring the White Pages

Materials

- white pages of the telephone book for every two or three students
- writing materials

Activity

Divide your class into groups of two or three. Have students browse through the front of a phone book and make a list of all the information they find: maps, community services, local attractions, things to do, sports and performing arts, and so on. Compare lists. Have students find their own home listings, too.

Day 3—Exploring the Yellow Pages

Materials

- yellow pages of the telephone book for every two or three students
- writing materials

Activity

Divide your class into small groups of two or three. Have students browse through the front of a phone book and make a list of local toy stores, frozen yogurt restaurants, pizza deliveries, and any other categories that you think might interest them. Compare lists.

Day 4—Current Technology

Materials

- a cellular phone and/or a pager

Activity

If you have a cellular phone and/or a pager, demonstrate their use. If you don't have these available, ask a friend or colleague to come in and demonstrate them. Make sure students know how to page someone.

Background

The first patent for false teeth was granted on March 9, 1822. The history of false teeth stretches back for centuries, however. Hearing this history can be a good incentive for keeping one's real teeth healthy through careful cleaning, regular dental care, and wearing braces, if necessary.

Making It Work

Try to arrange to have a dentist, dental hygienist, or the school nurse come visit your class on Thursday of this week to present a culminating activity. Some schools have supplies of toothbrushes and toothpaste for presentations of this kind, as well as models of teeth for demonstrations of brushing and so on.

Day 1—Different Kinds of Teeth

Materials

- small individual hand mirrors

Activity

Have children examine their own teeth with a mirror as you give them this information:

- Everybody grows two sets of teeth: primary (or "baby") teeth and permanent teeth.

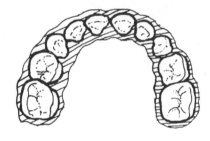

- There are 20 primary (or baby) teeth and 32 permanent teeth.

- The top and bottom sets of teeth fit into each other.

- The primary teeth consist of two central incisors in the front.

- On either side of the central incisors are the lateral incisors.

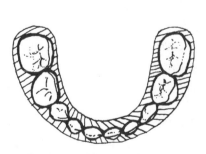

- On either side of the lateral incisors are the canine, or "eye," teeth. They are pointed.

- Behind the canines on either side of the mouth are the first molars and the second molars.

- The first permanent teeth to come in are the six-year molars. They come in back of the primary second molars.

- The next permanent teeth are the front ones, the central incisors. The baby teeth fall out to make room for them.

Day 2—The History of Dentistry

Materials

- encyclopedias or other illustrated reference materials

Activity

Have a whole-class discussion of the history of dentistry. Give the students these facts. Some students may want to do more research on their own.

- Archaeologists have discovered that prehistoric people used both magic and medicine to deal with the pain caused by decaying teeth. The ancient Etruscans made dental bridges—devices to hold false teeth in place—out of gold. These gold dental bridges have been found in Etruscan ruins.

- After the invention of writing, the Egyptians and Babylonians recorded their methods for treating teeth. There are references to treating and pulling teeth in Greek medical scrolls written as far back as 600 years B.C.

- During the Middle Ages, barbers were also dentists as well as doctors, and jewelers made dentures or false teeth.

- It wasn't until 1840 that the first dental school was established in Baltimore, Maryland.

- Much progress was made in dentistry after the discovery of the x-ray and the development of anesthesia.

Day 3—Braces

Materials

- student volunteers from your own class or borrowed from another class

Activity

Tell students that the way their teeth come together, or their "bite," is very important to dental health. If it looks as though a person's bite is going to be wrong, a dentist may suggest braces. Dentists who specialize in straightening teeth are called orthodontists.

Have student volunteers show their braces and describe their experiences. Some students may want to ask questions.

Day 4—A Visit from a Dental Professional

Materials

- Your visiting dental professional may bring materials to give out to the students.

Activity

Ask your dental professional to speak to the students about his or her specialty as well as to instruct them in the proper way of caring for their teeth.

Day 5—Tooth Care Chart

Materials

- copies of the chart, below
- small reward stickers, if desired

Activity

Review proper tooth brushing and send the chart home with the students. Provide extras for students who want to continue keeping a record.

Name _____   Date _____

Tooth Care Chart			
Date	A.M./P.M.	Date	A.M./P.M.

St. Patrick's
Day

Background

Saint Patrick died on March 17, 492 A.D. As a boy, he had been captured by Irish raiders and taken to Ireland as a slave. Later, he became a priest and spent years in an English monastery. He then returned to Ireland to preach Christianity and thereafter was made a bishop. After his death, he was declared the patron saint of Ireland. The anniversary of his death is celebrated all over the world, wherever immigrants have settled.

Making It Work

Show a film or video of the Irish countryside or read the book *St. Patrick's Day in the Morning* by Eve Bunting (Houghton Mifflin, 1983). The illustrations will help students picture the setting of this green country.

Day 1—Ireland

Materials

- classroom wall map of the world
- individual outline maps of Great Britain for each student (See below.)

Activity

Have students find (or help them locate) Great Britain on the world map. Note its position in relation to the United States. Then find Ireland and note its position in relation to the rest of Great Britain. Have students label England and Ireland on their outline maps and mark some of the principal cities.

Day 2—Irish Immigrants

Materials

- encyclopedias or other illustrated reference materials

Activity

This is designed to be an oral exercise to establish a general base of information. See what the students already know and tell them the answers they don't know. Repeat some of the questions and answers for reinforcement.

- The United States is home to millions of people who either were born in Ireland or are descendants of people who were born there.
- During the potato famine of the 1840s, hundreds of thousands of people left Ireland.
- Some early Irish immigrants moved west as pioneers.
- Many Irish immigrants settled on the east coast and entered politics and public service.
- Other Irish immigrants worked on the transcontinental railroad.

Day 3—Wearin' of the Green

Materials

- white or manila drawing paper
- shamrocks cut from heavy paper (enlarge pattern on page 38)
- crayons in all shades of green

Activity

Tell students that green is Ireland's color. For many years, the Irish were forbidden by English law to wear green, and now they are very enthusiastic about wearing it. As a matter of fact, lots of people wear green on St. Patrick's Day, even if they aren't Irish. The shamrock with its three green leaves is another symbol associated with St. Patrick.

Trace shamrocks in overlapping patterns on drawing paper. Color with all shades of green. Or shape shamrocks out of paper and decorate each one differently— stripes, dots, swirls—in shades of green. Display them on a bulletin board.

Day 3—Wearin' of the Green (cont.)

Day 4—Leprechauns

Materials

- writing and drawing materials

Activity

Tell students about leprechauns, the imaginary "little people" of Ireland. According to legend, each leprechaun has a pot of gold hidden somewhere. If you can catch a leprechaun, he will give you his pot of gold in exchange for his freedom. But leprechauns are very tricky and hard to catch!

Have students write or dictate stories called "How to Catch a Leprechaun." Ask students to illustrate their stories.

Day 5—St. Pat's Party

Materials

- party supplies
- green cupcakes or cookies and punch

Activity

Have a St. Patrick's Day party. Let each student share his or her leprechaun story and illustration as part of the entertainment.

Background

The first day of spring usually occurs on March 21. It is the day when the sun is directly above the equator and the hours of daylight are exactly equal to the hours of darkness. Another name for the first day of spring is the vernal equinox. Since the seasons are reversed below the equator, the first day of spring in the northern hemisphere is the first day of fall in the southern hemisphere.

Making It Work

Make the season a firsthand experience for your students by going for a nature walk to observe the signs of spring: nesting birds, new plant growth, blossoms, etc.

Day 1—Nature Walk

Materials

- copies of observation form below

Activity

Go for a nature walk around your school or neighborhood. Even in the most urban environment, you will see budding trees and returning birds.

Name _____   Date _____

Nature Walk Observation Form

What I Saw	Where I Saw It

Day 2—Spring Words Brainstorm

Materials

- writing materials

Activity

As a large-group activity, have students brainstorm as many words as possible having to do
with spring. Write the words on the chalkboard and have students copy them for use in the
next activity. They should have at least 20 words. Here are some suggestions:

- buds
- flowers
- blossoms
- birds
- nests
- rain
- puddles

- clouds
- showers
- nature
- warm
- thaw
- kites
- wind

- breeze
- caterpillars
- butterflies
- lambs
- kittens
- growth

Materials

- list of spring brainstorm words
- graph paper

Activity

Show students how to use their lists of words to lay out a word search puzzle. Show them
the example below. Then fill in other letters.

	B	U	T	T	E	R	F	L	I	E	S		N	E	S	T	S
F	L	O	W	E	R	S				H	B	R	E	E	Z	E
N	O		B	U	D	S			C	L	O	U	D	S			T
A	S		I	L		W	G	R	O	W	T	H					I
T	S		R	A	I	N	I			E							K
U	O		D	M		N			R						
R	M		S	B	P	U	D	D	L	E	S	W	A	R	M
E	S														
			C	A	T	E	R	P	I	L	L	A	R	S

Day 4—Writing a Spring Poem

Materials

- writing materials
- poetry collection for children

Activity

Read some poems aloud to your class to get them in the mood for writing poetry.

Remind them that poems may or may not rhyme.

Show them how to count the beats (rhythm) in a few lines of familiar poetry by marking the words that are naturally stressed.

> Jáck and Jill went úp the hill
> To fétch a páil of wáter.

Suggest that they use their lists of spring words to help them get started.

Be sure to tell students that they will probably need to try a few drafts to write their poems the way they want them and that it's all right to scratch out and rewrite. They can copy (and illustrate) their final versions on Friday.

Day 5—Copying and Illustrating a Spring Poem

Materials

- paper with room for a poem and illustration
- crayons

Activity

Allow plenty of time for students to copy and illustrate their spring poems. Display the completed work on a bulletin board.

Background

There are many stories about the origin of April Fool's Day. It is similar to the ancient Roman festival of Hilaria and to the Hindu festival of Holi. Our April Fool's Day may have gotten its start when the adoption of the Gregorian calendar caused the date of the New Year to change from spring to winter. Today, April 1, is a time for playing tricks on people. It is celebrated in much the same way in the United States, Canada, and Great Britain.

Making It Work

Help your students think up "safe and sane" tricks to play. Publish a "Nonsense Newspaper." Make cards and tell jokes. You can even do some research and an art project.

Day 1—Nonsense Newspaper

Materials

- a computer with word processing capability and a printer
- paper

Activity

Give your students some background on April Fool's Day and suggest writing a Nonsense Newspaper to fool another class. Have each person write or dictate funny news items. Make sure students understand that these stories should not be written to embarrass or harm anyone else. If this is a concern, have students write their items about themselves. A good example might be something like this:

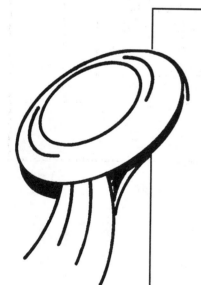

Flying Saucer Sighted

The flying saucer noticed yesterday by many students on the roof of the school office turned out to be a paper plate. It was launched by a student who had finished his lunch and tried to sail his trash into the nearby trash can. Better practice that shot!

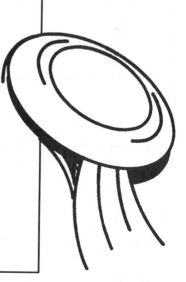

Enter everyone's news items (or let them enter their own) and print the newspaper for distribution to another class on April Fool's Day.

Day 2—Surprise Cards

Materials

- construction paper
- scissors
- glue
- crayons and/or markers

Activity

Make pop-out surprise cards by pleating a strip of construction paper, adding a jack-in-the-box head and folding it down inside a card. When the card is opened, the jack-in-the-box will pop out. (See illustrations below.)

fold and tuck inside

Day 3—Joke Time

Materials

- an assortment of children's joke books

Activity

Ask each student to tell or read a favorite joke to the class. Take time to laugh.

Day 4—Research Time

Materials

- encyclopedias or other illustrated reference materials

Activity

Have students complete the following questions on separate paper to find out about the Hindu festival of Holi.

Holi

1. What kind of holiday is Holi?

2. Why do children love it?

3. How long does the celebration last?

4. What special foods are eaten?

5. What is the religious reason for Holi?

Answers:

1. It is a holiday that celebrates the beginning of spring.

2. They get to throw colored water at everybody.

3. The celebration lasts three days.

4. Special candies are eaten.

5. It commemorates the time when Krishna came to earth and played with the colors of life.

Day 5—Tempera Time

Materials

- powdered tempera and water
- paper for painting
- brushes, if desired

Activity

Mix up "colored water" and have children create pictures with fingers or brushes to celebrate your own version of Holi.

Background

On April 13, 1796, the first elephant ever seen in the United States was brought from Bengal, India, to New York City. The most famous elephant, however, was Jumbo. P. T. Barnum bought Jumbo from the London Zoo in 1882 for his circus. Today elephants are on the list of endangered animals.

Making It Work

Ask how many of your students have seen a live elephant in a circus or zoo. Have any of them ridden on an elephant's back? Share experiences and information.

Day 1—Facts about Elephants

Materials

- encyclopedias or other illustrated reference materials

Activity

This activity is designed to be an oral exercise to establish a general knowledge base. See what the students already know and tell them the answers they don't know. Repeat questions about the information for reinforcement.

- The elephant is the largest land animal. Of all the animals, only the whale is bigger.
- The elephant has the largest ears of all animals and the biggest teeth (tusks).
- An elephant's skin is about an inch thick, but since they do not have a layer of fat under their skin they are very sensitive to cold.
- The elephant is the only animal with a nose in the shape of a trunk. The tip of the trunk is very flexible and enables the elephants to pick up small objects. The trunk itself is very strong. An elephant can easily pick up a 600-pound (270 kg) log with its trunk.
- An elephant's long curved tusks are its incisors. They are made of ivory. An elephant can pick up a load weighing a ton (2,000 lbs/900 kg) with its tusks.

- An elephant only has four molars at any time, two on the top and two on the bottom. They are about one foot (30 cm) long and weigh about 8 pounds (3.6 kg) each. During its lifetime, an elephant grows six sets of molars.
- An elephant weighs about 200 pounds (90 kg) and stands about 3 feet (.9 m) tall at birth.

Day 2—Two Kinds of Elephants

Materials

- encyclopedias or other illustrated reference materials
- classroom wall map of the world

Activity

Have students consult reference books to contrast the two kinds of elephants: African elephants and Asian or Indian elephants.

Name _____   Date _____

Two Kinds of Elephants		
	African	**Indian**
Height		
Ears		
Trunk		
Tusk		
Back		
Color		

Day 3—Working Elephants

Materials

- encyclopedias or other illustrated reference materials

Activity

In many parts of the world, elephants were (and sometimes still are) used to doing heavy work. Have students find out how these animals were captured and trained and what kinds of work they did or still do.

Day 4—Zoos and Circuses

Materials

- encyclopedias or other illustrated reference materials

Activity

Discuss the ethics of zoos and circuses with your students. Many people feel that elephants should not be kept in captivity or trained to entertain people. Other people feel that it is all right to use elephants in these ways as long as they are treated well and not kept in small cages. People who run zoos and circuses try to make natural environments for the elephants to live in. Many of these people believe that there is no other way for most people to see elephants.

Have your students write or dictate their opinions about this subject. Let students share their opinions and discuss them. You can tally the opinions and make a variety of graphic representations.

Day 5—Endangered Animals

Materials

- encyclopedias or other illustrated reference materials

Activity

Have students make personal lists of the animals they think are endangered and why. Compile this information into a master list. Let student volunteers go to the library and check this information for the class.

Name _____ Date _____

Endangered Animals		
Animal	**Country**	**Reason**

Background

On April 18, 1934, the first laundromat opened in Fort Worth, Texas. This was a great convenience for people who did not have washing machines at home. The laundromat has become a staple of life in the United States. People who do not want to invest in a washing machine, don't have room for one, or are traveling make use of laundromats.

Making It Work

Ask your students if they ever help do the laundry. Ask what they think it would have been like to do the laundry in pioneer days. See if they know where soap comes from.

Day 1—How Soap Is Made

Materials

- encyclopedias or other illustrated reference materials

Activity

This activity is designed to be an oral exercise to establish a general knowledge base. See what the students already know and tell them the answers they don't know. Repeat questions about the information for reinforcement.

- The word "detergent" once meant any substance used for cleaning. "Detergent" has come to mean a synthetic (artificial, manmade) substance that acts like soap.

- In general, soap is made by boiling oils or fats with alkalis. Alkali solutions are sometimes called lye.

- Adding soap or detergent to water makes the water "wetter" and better able to penetrate dirt and grease (wetting action).

- Soap or detergent breaks oil and grease into small droplets (emulsifying action).

- Soap or detergent breaks dirt into fine particles that are suspended in water (dispersing action).

- Soap or detergent is helped to work better by rubbing, squeezing, or agitating (moving) whatever is being washed.

- Detergents do not leave a "scum" like soap, and they work in cold water.

Day 2—Soap Making in Pioneer Days

Materials

- encyclopedias or other illustrated reference materials

Activity

Depending on the age group you are teaching, help students find the answers to these questions or let them do their own research.

1. Where did the American pioneers get their soap?

2. About how often did they renew their supply?

3. Where did the soap makers get the oils and fats they needed?

4. How was lye produced?

5. What was the soap like?

- -

Answers:

1. They made their own.
2. They made soap once a year.
3. They saved fats and grease from cooking and butchering.
4. Wood ashes were saved in a barrel. Water was poured through them and trickled out a hole near the bottom. The resulting liquid was lye.
5. The soap was yellow and soft like jelly.

Day 3—The History of the Washing Machine

Materials

- encyclopedias or other illustrated reference materials
- large paper or poster board
- art materials

Activity

Depending on the age group you are teaching, help students find the information they need or let them do their own research.

Have students create posters tracing the development of the washing machine through history. (Suggestions: flat rocks in a stream, washboards and tubs, mechanical devices, electric machines with wringers, automatic washers)

Day 4—What's Different?

Materials

- writing materials

Activity

Have students write, or dictate to you or an instructional assistant, the differences they see between doing the laundry today and in pioneer days. Compare the kind of soap or detergent used, where the soap or detergent comes from, how the clothes are actually washed and dried, and the amount of time everything takes.

Day 5—Soap Sculpture

Materials

- large bars of soft white soap
- carving tools (dull knives like the ones sold for carving jack-o-lanterns, orangewood sticks, etc.)
- paper and pencils
- carbon paper

Activity

Spread newspaper out on desks. Give each student an unwrapped bar of soap and carving tools. Have students think of something to make that will fit the shape of the bar. A boat is a good choice because it is an easy shape, and if made from Ivory soap, it will float. An animal like a bear will work, too.

Students should make a sketch of the side view of an animal or the top view of a boat. They can transfer these sketches to the soap with carbon paper. Advise them to scrape off a little of the soap at a time and to keep turning their sculpture from side to side as they work. The completed carving can be smoothed and polished with a tissue or paper towel.

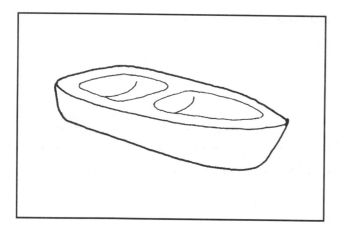

Background

Arbor Day is celebrated on different days in different states but usually at the end of April or the beginning of May. It was first celebrated in Nebraska in 1872 when a settler named Julius Sterling Morton persuaded his state to set aside a day for tree planting in order to preserve the topsoil of the prairie. On that first Arbor Day more than a million trees were planted.

Making It Work

Since the date for celebrating this occasion varies so widely, you can choose any day in late April that is convenient for you. Celebrating Arbor Day by planting one or more trees at school is appropriate because that is one of the few ways that children can actually help to improve the environment.

Day 1—Writing Letters

Materials

- writing materials

Activity

Check with your principal and then plan to invite parents and other classes to a tree-planting ceremony on Friday of the week you choose for your celebration. Ask a local nursery to donate a tree (or buy a small one yourself). Have students write letters of invitation to their parents and to other classes.

Day 2—Gifts from the Trees

Materials

- construction paper in brown and green
- crayons or fine-line black markers
- scissors
- tree made from brown construction paper (see page 52)
- leaf patterns (see page 52)
- bulletin board space

Activity

Cut a large tree trunk and branches from brown construction paper and attach it to a bulletin board with the heading "Gifts from the Trees." Have each student cut out one or more leaves from green construction paper and write on each leaf something that trees do for us or that we get from trees. Attach the leaves to the tree.

Day 2—Gifts from the Trees *(cont.)*

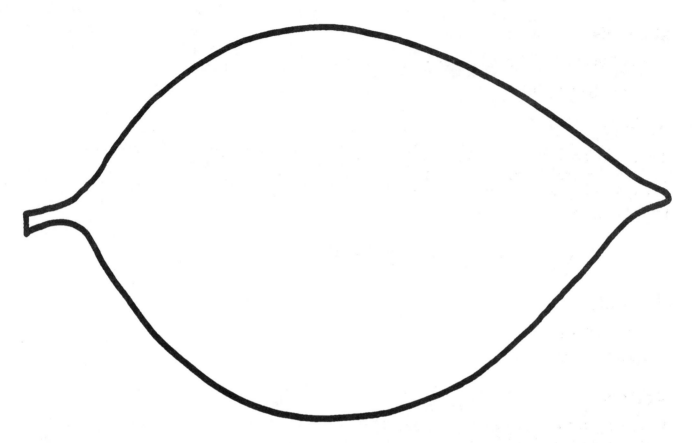

Day 3—Preparing the Program

Materials

- access to school library or a large selection of books of poetry
- writing materials

Activity

If possible, go to the library and allow students to browse through books to find poems they would like to memorize and present at your Arbor Day ceremony. Have each student copy the poem he or she would like to use. Remind them to note titles and authors. Send poems home to memorize for homework.

Day 4—Preparing the Program (cont.)

Materials

- poems copied yesterday
- art materials
- writing materials

Activity

Have students recopy their poems and decorate the margins of the paper with appropriate symbols of Arbor Day. They can carry these copies at the ceremony in case they forget their lines and later post them around the tree on the bulletin board. If you have extra time, let students practice reciting their poems.

Day 5—Presenting the Program

Materials

- tree
- planting tools
- water
- previously prepared poems

Activity

See if you can get someone (custodian, parent, older student) to dig the hole for your tree ahead of time. Then, with students gathered around, plant the tree. Each student can add a trowel full of dirt. When the tree is planted, have each student recite his or her poem. Have a lovely day!

Background

The Empire State Building in New York City was opened on May 1, 1931. It was the tallest building in the world until the opening of the World Trade Center in 1972, also in New York City.

Making It Work

Involve students in doing some research about architecture throughout history.

Day 1—Buildings in Ancient Egypt: The Great Pyramid

Materials

- encyclopedias or other illustrated reference materials
- questions below, reproduced for students

Activity

Have students find and record facts about the following questions:

1. When was the Great Pyramid built?
2. Where is it located?
3. How tall is it now?
4. What was its original height?
5. What is the area of its base?
6. What was it designed to be used for?

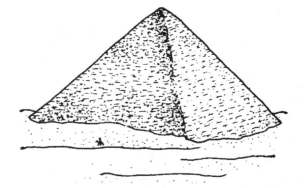

Answers: 1. During the 2600s B.C.; 2. Near the Nile River outside the city of Cairo in Egypt; 3. About 450 ft. (130 m) above the ground; 4. About 481 ft. (144 m)—the capstone has fallen off ; 5. Its base covers about 15 acres. (6 hectares) ; 6. It was built to serve as a tomb for the Pharaoh Khufu (also called Cheops).

Day 2—Buildings in Ancient Greece: The Parthenon

Materials

- encyclopedias or other illustrated reference materials
- questions on top of page 55, reproduced for students

Day 2—Buildings in Ancient Greece: The Parthenon *(cont.)*

Activity

Have students find and record the facts about the following questions.

1. When was the Parthenon completed?

2. Where is it located?

3. What were its outside dimensions?

4. What was its original purpose?

Answers: 1. 438 B.C.; 2. On the Acropolis at Athens, Greece; 3. 228 feet (68 m) long, 101 feet (30 m) wide, 60 feet (18 m) high; 4. To honor Athena Parthenos, the patron goddess of Athens

Day 3—Buildings in Ancient Rome: The Colosseum

Materials

- encyclopedias or other illustrated reference materials
- questions below, reproduced for students

Activity

Have students find and record the facts about the following questions.

1. When was the Colosseum completed?

2. Where is it located?

3. What are its outside dimensions?

4. How many spectators could be seated?

Answers: 1. 80 A.D.; 2. Near the center of present-day Rome; 3. 161 feet high, 600 feet long, 500 feet wide; 4. About 45,000

Day 4—Buildings in Medieval Europe: Cathedral of Saint Mark

Materials

- encyclopedias or other illustrated reference materials
- questions below, reproduced for students

Activity

Have students find and record the facts about the following questions.

1. When was work on this cathedral begun?
2. Where is it located?
3. In what form is the building and what are its dimensions?
4. It is an example of what kind of architecture?

Answers: 1. 1050 A.D.; 2. In Venice, Italy; 3. The building is in the form of a Greek cross, 250 feet (75 m) long and 220 feet (66 m) wide; 4. Byzantine architecture

---

Day 5—Modern American Skyscrapers: The Empire State Building

Materials

- encyclopedias or other illustrated reference materials
- questions below, reproduced for students

Activity

Have students find and record the facts about the following questions.

1. When was the Empire State Building opened?
2. Where is it located?
3. How many stories does it have?
4. What is its total height including the TV tower?

Answers: 1. 1931 A.D.; 2. On Fifth Avenue in New York City; 3. 102 stories; 4. 1,472 feet (442 m), more than a quarter of a mile high

---

Background

At one time in Japan, Boys' Day was celebrated on May 5, while girls had a special celebration of their own in March called the Festival of Dolls. Now, however, May 5 is a day for both boys and girls. On that day, Japanese parents honor their children and take them to Shinto shrines to be blessed by the priests.

Making It Work

Show a film or video tape on Japan. Try to get one that features traditional dress and ceremonies and includes scenes of the countryside as well as the big cities.

Day 1—The Carp as a Symbol

Materials

- paper cups
- markers
- crepe paper
- crayons
- string
- stapler

Activity

Tell students about the meaning of the carp. (It symbolizes the courage parents want for their children because it swims upstream against the current.) Make carp kites for the students to take home. Draw the carp's face on the cup (see below). Staple streamers cut from crepe paper to the open end of the cup. Make four holes in the bottom of the paper cup (the carp's nose) and thread the strings through. Tie the ends together.

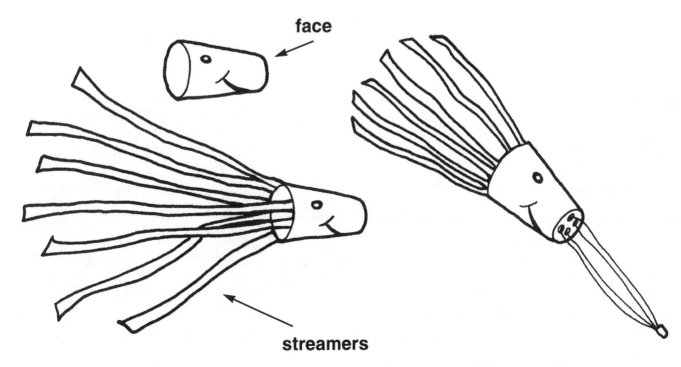

face

streamers

Day 2—Origami: Japanese Paper Folding

Materials

- special origami paper or lightweight white paper cut in squares
- a book about origami

Activity

Give each student one or more pieces of paper. Read aloud the directions for a simple example of origami and have everyone follow along at the same time. Some students will find this a fascinating activity. Leave the book and some paper in an activity center for individual exploration of this art form.

Day 3—Origami: *Sadako and the Thousand Paper Cranes*

Materials

- *Sadako and the Thousand Paper Cranes* by Eleanor Coerr

Activity

Read this book aloud to your class. Discuss the story. Have students write or dictate their feelings about the story.

Try folding paper cranes. Consult your book on origami for directions. Estimate how long it would take your class to fold one thousand paper cranes.

Day 4—Festival of Dolls

Materials

- dolls brought from home

Activity

Just as only boys once made carp kites, only girls celebrated the Festival of Dolls. However, girls can now share the carp as a symbol of courage and boys can own dolls, although they may think of them as "action figures." Have students clear off shelves in the classroom and plan to bring dolls to school for the culminating activity of their Children's Day celebration on Friday.

Day 5—Haiku Party

Materials

- dolls on display
- haiku worksheet below
- almond cookies or Japanese rice snacks
- tea (use punch and pretend)

Activity

Have a party honoring the visiting dolls. Each student should write (or dictate) a tribute to his or her doll or action figure. Show students how to clap or tap and count syllables before they start writing. When the poems are complete, ask each student to read his or her poem aloud.

Name _____ Date _____

Writing Haiku

A haiku poem has three lines made up of 17 syllables.

There are 5 syllables in the first line, 7 syllables in the second line, and 5 syllables in the third line.

The lines do not need to rhyme.

Here are two examples:

> G.I. Joe is strong. (5)
> He wears a green uniform. (7)
> He can win battles. (5)

> My doll's name is Belle. (5)
> She looks a lot like I do. (7)
> She has brown skin, too. (5)

Now write your own haiku. Use the back of this paper to write more than one.

(5) _____

(7) _____

(5) _____

Background

Mother's Day is celebrated on the second Sunday in May. It was first celebrated in the United States in 1872 as a Mother's Day for Peace, as suggested by Julia Ward Howe. She had nursed the wounded during the Civil War and was dedicated to the cause of peace. She is best known for writing "The Battle Hymn of the Republic." In 1907, Anna Jarvis started a campaign for a national Mother's Day. In 1915, President Wilson declared the second Sunday in May to be Mother's Day in the United States.

Making It Work

Ask students how they celebrate Mother's Day. Are other female family members such as grandmothers and aunts honored too? Do any of their customs come from another culture or country?

Day 1—Mother's Day Around the World

Materials

- encyclopedias or other illustrated reference materials
- writing materials
- "Mother's Day Around the World" research form below

Activity

Help students find information about how mothers are honored in different countries or let them do research on their own.

Name _____ Date _____

Mother's Day Around The World

Country _____

Customs _____

_____

_____

Country _____

Customs _____

_____

_____

Day 2—My Mother: An Essay

Materials

- writing materials

Activity

Have each student write (or dictate to you or an instructional assistant) an essay titled "My Mother." Help students edit and complete final copies of their work to present to their mothers for Mother's Day. Or, have a bulletin board display titled "Our Mothers" and post these essays for all to see and read. (If a student does not have a mother, encourage him or her to write about another female loved one.)

Day 3—Mother's Day Cards

Materials

- art supplies
- paper or copy of card below

Activity

Have students make cards based on the word "Mother."

M is for _____

O is for _____

T is for _____

H is for _____

E is for _____

R is for _____

Put them all together; they spell Mother!

Day 4—Coupon Books

Materials

- paper
- writing materials
- art supplies

Activity

Have students make and illustrate personalized coupons that can be stapled into book form. They can include coupons for things that would be particularly meaningful to their own mothers.

Happy Mother's Day

Good for

_____

_____

_____

_____

_____

_____

Day 5—Breakfast Plans

Materials

- writing materials

Activity

Since many children believe mother wants breakfast in bed more than anything else, go over plans for this project with them. Talk about serving it on a tray and including eating utensils and napkins. Caution them to get an adult to help with any actual cooking or coffee making!

Background

On May 29, 1790, Rhode Island became the 13th state to ratify the Constitution. Although it was the first colony to declare its independence from Great Britain, it was the last to sign the Constitution because it insisted on amendments that protected the rights of small states. Rhode Island has maintained the distinction of being the smallest state in the Union. Although students have little exposure to American history at this age, it is fun to learn interesting facts about the states.

Making It Work

Tell the students that this week they will be learning a little bit about Rhode Island, the smallest of the United States.

Day 1—Tracing Rhode Island

Materials

- classroom wall map of the United States

Activity

Use tracing paper to draw the outline of Rhode Island from the wall map. Transfer this outline to heavier paper and cut out several Rhode Islands. Ask students to estimate how many times Rhode Island will fit into the state they live in and into any or all of the other states. (If you live in Rhode Island, let students choose the states to compare it to.)

After your estimates (guesses) have been made, let volunteers take turns actually fitting the traced map of Rhode Island into the boundaries of the states. Compare results.

Name _____ Date _____

Rhode Island Guess and Check		
Name of State	**Guess**	**Check**

Day 2—Just the Facts

Materials

- encyclopedias or other illustrated reference materials
- classroom wall map of the United States

Activity

This is designed to be an oral exercise to establish a general base of information. See what the students already know and tell them the information they don't know. Repeat some of the questions and answers for reinforcement.

- The colony of Rhode Island was founded by Roger Williams in 1636 for the purpose of establishing religious freedom.
- Rhode Island was the first colony to declare its independence from Great Britain.
- On May 29, 1790, Rhode Island became the 13th state to ratify the Constitution.
- Rhode Island has the distinction of being the smallest state in the Union.
- Rhode Island has an area of 1,214 square miles (3035 km²).
- Rhode Island's greatest distance north to south is 48 miles (80 km); the greatest distance, east to west is 37 miles (62 km).
- Since 1901, Providence has been the capital of Rhode Island. (Find it on the map.)

Day 3—State Flowers, State Trees

Materials

- encyclopedias or other illustrated reference materials

Activity

Continue the chart below to compare the state flower and tree of Rhode Island with the state flowers and trees of various states of your choice.

Name _____   Date _____

State Name	State Flower	State Tree
Rhode Island		

Day 4—More Facts

Materials

- encyclopedias or other illustrated reference materials

Activity

Depending on the age group you are teaching, help students answer these questions or have them use research materials on their own.

Name _____   Date _____

1. What is Rhode Island's state bird? _____

2. What is Rhode Island's state motto? _____

3. What is the highest point in Rhode Island? _____

4. What is the lowest point in Rhode Island? _____

5. What is the name of the statue on top of the state's capitol? _____

- -

Answers:

1. The state bird is the Rhode Island Red, a type of chicken.
2. "Hope" is the state motto.
3. The highest point is Jerimoth Hill, 812 feet (244 m) above sea level.
4. The lowest point is at sea level along the Atlantic Ocean.
5. The statue's name is Independent Man.

Day 5—Opinions

Materials

- writing materials

Activity

Depending upon the size of the state you live in, ask students to write about (or dictate to you or an instructional assistant) the good and bad points of their living situation. Does the size of the state make a difference in the way people live? Or are other things—such as climate, location, wealth, natural resources, and so on more important? Share everyone's ideas and have a discussion.

Background

Ice cream was first advertised and sold in the United States on June 8, 1786. Some people say ice cream was known and eaten in ancient Rome. Others say the first ice cream was made in Italy in about 1550. However, it wasn't until the end of the eighteenth century that it became available in stores.

Making It Work

Read *Ice Cream* by William Jaspherson (Macmillan, 1988) or *The Scoop on Ice Cream* by Vicki Cobb (Little, Brown, 1985) to your class to get them interested.

Day 1—Fun Facts about Ice Cream

Materials

- encyclopedias or other illustrated reference materials
- *Ice Cream* by William Jaspherson (Macmillan, 1988)
- *The Scoop on Ice Cream* by Vicki Cobb (Little, Brown, 1985)

Activity

This activity is designed to be an oral exercise to establish a general base of entertaining information. See what the students already know and tell them the information they don't know. Repeat some of the questions and answers for reinforcement.

- Some people say ice cream was known and eaten in ancient Rome.

- Others say the first ice cream was made in Italy in about 1550.

- Ice cream was a favorite dessert in George and Martha Washington's home at Mount Vernon.

- Ice cream was first served in the White House by Dolly Madison.

- Ice cream became commercially available in the United States in the late eighteenth century.

- Baltimore, Maryland, claims to be the birthplace of the ice cream industry.

- Ice cream cones were first sold at the World's Fair in St. Louis, Missouri, in 1904.

- More ice cream is consumed in the United States than in any other country.

Day 2—Brainstorming Descriptive Words

Materials

- Brainstorming form below

Activity

As a large group, have your class brainstorm words that describe ice cream. Write the words on the board and then have students copy their favorites for use later in the week.

Day 3—Brainstorming Original Flavors

Materials

- Brainstorming form below

Activity

As a large group, have your class brainstorm original flavors for ice cream. Write the words on the board and then have students copy their favorites for use later in the week.

Name _____   Date _____

Brainstorming Form	
Descriptive Words	**Flavors**

Day 4—Write an Ice Cream Ad

Materials

- brainstorming sheets
- writing materials
- art materials

Activity

Have each student pick a flavor and, using a selection of descriptive words, write an ice cream advertisement to present to the class. Encourage students to create visual material to go along with their ads. These can take the form of advertising posters, newspaper or magazine ads, ice cream cartons, storyboards for TV spots—whatever they can dream up.

Day 5—Advertising Presentation

Materials

- student-made advertisements and visuals

Activity

Have each student present his or her ice cream advertisement to the class. Then, when all the presentations have been given, have students vote on the ice cream they would buy because of the ad. Give ribbons to all participants and an award to the winner.

Background

Explorers Marquette and Joliet were looking for a water route to the Pacific Ocean when they discovered on June 17, 1673, that the Mississippi River flowed into the Gulf of Mexico.

The river itself had been discovered in 1541 by Hernando De Soto near what is now Memphis, Tennessee.

Making It Work

The Mississippi River has played a great part in American history. It is interesting to learn some basic facts about this great river.

Day 1—Facts About the Mississippi

Materials

- encyclopedias or other illustrated reference materials
- classroom wall map of the United States

Activity

This is designed to be an oral exercise to establish a general base of information. See what the students already know and tell them the information they don't know. Repeat some of the questions and answers for reinforcement.

- The Mississippi was first sighted in 1541 by explorer Hernando De Soto near what is now Memphis, Tennessee.
- Explorers Marquette and Joliet were looking for a water route to the Pacific Ocean when they discovered on June 17, 1673, that the Mississippi River flowed into the Gulf of Mexico.
- The Mississippi winds about 2,350 miles (3,760 km) from its source near the United States border with Canada, to its mouth in the Gulf of Mexico.
- Together with its tributary, the Missouri River, it makes up one of the largest river systems in the world, about 3,710 miles (5,936 km).
- The Mississippi forms a major part of the largest inland waterway in the world, from the St. Lawrence Seaway to the Gulf of Mexico. (Find on map.)
- The Mississippi formed the western boundary of the United States when Jefferson became President in 1801. (Find on map.)
- Jefferson's Louisiana Purchase extended the territory of the United States from the Mississippi River westward to the Rocky Mountains.
- The Mississippi has been celebrated in song and story by people as diverse as Mark Twain (*The Adventures of Tom Sawyer, Huckleberry Finn, Life on the Mississippi*) and George Gershwin (*Porgy and Bess*).

Day 2—Discovery by Accident

Materials

- encyclopedias or other illustrated reference materials
- classroom wall map of the United States
- classroom globe

Activity

Tell students that Marquette and Joliet were not the only explorers to discover one important thing while looking for something else. See if they can answer the questions below and then demonstrate their answers by using the map or the globe.

Name _____ Date _____

1. What was Columbus looking for when he discovered America? _____

   _____

2. Why was his trip important to the Europeans of his time? _____

   _____

3. Where did Columbus land? _____

   _____

4. What did he call the native people he found? _____

   Why? _____

5. Why wasn't he able to get where he had planned to go? _____

   _____

Answers:

1. He was trying to reach the East Indies, the Spice Islands.
2. They needed spices to preserve their food, and the overland routes were made too dangerous by bandits.
3. He landed on an island in the Bahamas that he named San Salvador.
4. Columbus called the native people Indians because he thought he had reached the East Indies.
5. Columbus was not able to get where he had planned to go because the continents of North and South America were in his way.

Day 3—Mississippi Stern-wheelers

Materials

- encyclopedias or other illustrated reference materials
- paper
- writing materials
- art materials

Activity

Help students find information about the Mississippi River boats called sternwheelers. Have them work in cooperative groups to turn this information into drawings of this unique kind of boat. Some students may wish to try making a model instead of a picture.

Have students write about the uses for this boat, some of which were unique. When the pictures and written pieces are complete, ask students to compare their information with the whole class.

Day 4—Tom and Huck

Materials

- *The Adventures of Tom Sawyer* in movie or book form

Activity

Try to get a video of the classic *Tom Sawyer* movie. Show the whole film if you have time or pre-select scenes that will give students a glimpse of the Mississippi.

If you can't get the movie or don't have time to show it, read selections from Mark Twain's *Tom Sawyer* aloud to your students.

Day 5—"Old Man River"

Materials

- a recording of "Old Man River" from Gershwin's opera, *Porgy and Bess*

Activity

Play "Old Man River" for the students as a culmination of this week's mini-unit on the Mississippi River.

Background

On June 19, 1910, Father's Day was first celebrated in Spokane, Washington. It is now celebrated throughout the United States on the third Sunday in June, as recommended by President Calvin Coolidge.

Making It Work

Ask students how they celebrate Father's Day. Are other male family members such as grandfathers and uncles honored too? Do any of their customs come from another culture or country?

Day 1—Father's Day Cards

Materials

- art supplies
- paper or copy of card, below

Activity

Have students make cards based on the word "Father."

F is for _____

A is for _____

T is for _____

H is for _____

E is for _____

R is for _____

Put them all together; they spell FATHER!

Day 2—Father's Day Essay

Materials

- writing materials

Activity

Have each student write (or dictate to you or an instructional assistant) an essay titled "What Is Special about My Dad." Help students edit and complete final copies of their work to present to their fathers for Father's Day. As an alternative, create a bulletin board display titled "Our Dads," and post these essays for all to see and read. (If a student does not have a father, encourage him or her to write about another male loved one.)

Day 3—Father's Day Collage Card

Materials

- old magazines
- scissors, glue
- half sheets of construction paper
- pens or markers

Activity

Have students go through old magazines and cut out a selection of things that represent their father's interests, hobbies, sports, favorite foods, etc.

Help students arrange these pictures in collage form on their pieces of construction paper, moving them around and overlapping them until they get the effect they want. Show them how to carefully lift one piece at a time and glue it down until the whole card is done. Put a heavy book on top of the collage until it is flat and the glue is dry.

Fold the collage in half like a greeting card and write a message inside.

Collage

Fold the collage in half like a greeting card and write a message inside.

Day 4—Coupon Books

Materials

- paper
- writing materials
- art supplies

Activity

Fathers like coupon books, too! Have students make and illustrate personalized coupons that can be stapled into book form. They can include coupons for things that would be particularly meaningful to their own fathers.

Happy Father's Day

Good For

_____

_____

_____

_____

_____

_____

_____

_____

Day 5—Dinner Plans

Materials

- writing materials

Activity

Fathers may enjoy a special dinner more than breakfast in bed. Help students to think up a dinner menu that their fathers would like and that they could actually help prepare. Suggest that they show this menu to their mothers and offer to help with preparations and cleanup.

Background

On June 30, 1859, a French tightrope walker named Blondin topped all of the other daredevils who have risked their lives at Niagara Falls by walking a 1,100 feet (330 m) tightrope across the falls.

Making It Work

Why do people take risks? Have a whole class discussion about risk takers. What sports do they engage in? What careers do they enter? What do they get out of it?

Day 1—Niagara Falls Facts

Materials

- encyclopedias or other illustrated reference materials
- classroom wall map of the United States

Activity

This is designed to be an oral exercise to establish a general base of information. See what the students already know and tell them the information they don't know. Repeat some of the questions and answers for reinforcement. Stop and use the map as you go along.

- The Niagara River connects Lake Erie and Lake Ontario.

- It forms part of the boundary between New York and Ontario, Canada.

- The river splits and falls over a rocky gorge in two streams, forming Horseshoe Falls in Canada and the American Falls in New York.

- Horseshoe Falls are larger, 186 feet (56 m) high and 2,950 feet (885 m) wide at their widest point.

- The American Falls are 193 feet (58 m) high and about 1,400 feet (420 m) wide.

- People who want to see the falls from the bottom can take a ship called *The Maid of the Mist* around the river at the base of the falls.

- The shape of both falls changes periodically because the water wears away the underlying rock, which then falls into the river.

- About 500,000 tons (450,000 metric tons) of water a minute plunge over these two falls.

Day 2—Over the Falls

Materials

- encyclopedias or other illustrated reference materials
- research form below

Activity

Tell students that Niagara Falls has always attracted risk takers and daredevils. Blondin, the French tightrope walker who crossed the falls on June 30, 1859, was just one of many people who have risked their lives at Niagara Falls.

Go to the library as a group, if you can, and find out about all of the people who have tried stunts at Niagara Falls—their names, what they did, when they did it, and the results.

Name _____   Date _____

Niagara Risk Takers			
Who	**What**	**When**	**Result**

Day 3—Other Waterfalls

Materials

- encyclopedias or other illustrated reference materials
- classroom wall map of the world

Activity

Have students find out about other famous waterfalls in the world and locate them on the world map. Which is the highest? Where is it located? Try these:

Name _____ Date _____

Angel Falls _____

Victoria Falls _____

Bridalveil Falls _____

Day 4—Sports for Risk Takers

Materials

- encyclopedias or other illustrated reference materials

Activity

Brainstorm dangerous sports. Have each student write or dictate a description of the sport and the reason it might appeal to people. (Some suggestions are bungee jumping, hang gliding, mountain climbing, auto racing, and skydiving.)

Day 5—Careers for Risk Takers

Materials

- encyclopedias or other illustrated reference materials

Activity

Brainstorm dangerous careers. Have each student write or dictate a description of the career and the reason it might appeal to people. (Some suggestions are test pilots, fire fighters, and circus performers such as those who do their acts on trapezes and high wires.)

Background

The 4th of July, or Independence Day, is the birthday of our country. On this day in 1776, the Declaration of Independence was adopted by the Continental Congress. The day has traditionally been celebrated with ringing bells, fireworks, and patriotic speeches.

Making It Work

Get in the mood by playing patriotic music each morning and encouraging students to learn the lyrics.

Note: Have them sign up to bring red, white, and blue foods for Day 5.

Day 1—Ben and Me

Materials

- *Ben and Me* video

Activity

Show the video *Ben and Me* to get the students interested and start the week off with the appropriate patriotic flair.

Day 2—Heroes of the Revolutionary War

Materials

- encyclopedias or other illustrated reference materials

Activity

Help students find information about these important Revolutionary War figures or let them do the research on their own.

- George Washington
- Benjamin Franklin
- Patrick Henry
- Samuel Adams
- Paul Revere
- John Adams

Day 3—What about Fireworks?

Materials

- encyclopedias or other illustrated reference materials

Activity

Have students research and write the answers to these questions: When and where was gunpowder invented? What is the connection between gunpowder and fireworks? Which country used the first fireworks in its festivals and celebrations?

If fireworks are illegal in your area, review the reasons for the laws. If they are available, be sure to go over the safety rules associated with their use. Of course, the safest way to enjoy fireworks is to go to a public display. Most of these fireworks shows are put on by firefighters who are available in case any accidental fire occurs.

Day 4—My Favorite Fourth

Materials

- writing materials
- art supplies

Activity

Have each student write or dictate the way he or she best likes to spend the 4th of July. Ask them to include the foods they eat, where they go, what they do, and so on.

Help students edit and correct their stories and have them copy them on good paper with a space for an illustration at the top.

Post these illustrated stories on a bulletin board titled "My Favorite Fourth."

Day 5—Red, White, and Blue Party

Materials

- party supplies in red, white, and blue, if possible (You could have white plates, cups, and utensils on a "cloth" made of red or blue butcher or construction paper and use contrasting napkins.)
- red, white, and blue party food

Activity

Have students think of red foods (watermelon, strawberries, cherry pie, etc.).

Have students think of white foods. (vanilla ice cream, white cake with white icing, etc.)

Have students think of blue foods (blueberries, blue gelatin, etc.).

- Celebrate with a great party.
- Sing the patriotic songs you have learned.
- Share the "My Favorite Fourth" stories.

Background

The Liberty Bell, now kept in the Tower Room of Independence Hall in Philadelphia, Pennsylvania, was rung to announce the Declaration of Independence in 1776. The bell was rung every year thereafter until it cracked on July 8, 1835, during the funeral services for John Marshall, Chief Justice of the Supreme Court.

Making It Work

Talk about the symbols of the United States of America. The Liberty Bell is one. What are some others? Bells are important symbols in other countries, too.

Day 1—Fast Facts

Materials

- encyclopedias or other illustrated reference materials

Activity

Depending on the age group you are teaching, help students answer these questions or have them use research materials on their own.

Name _____ Date _____

1. How much does the Liberty Bell weigh? _____
2. How much did it cost originally?_____
3. Where was it first cast? _____
4. Why was it recast in 1753? _____
5. For how many years was it rung on Independence Day? _____
6. When did the Liberty Bell crack? _____
7. Can it still be rung? _____

- -

Answers:

1. The Liberty Bell weights more than 2,080 pounds (936 kg).
2. It cost $300 in 1752.
3. The bell was first cast in England.
4. It broke when it was rung after its arrival from England.
5. It rang for 59 years, from 1775 until 1835.
6. The bell cracked on July 8, 1835, during John Marshall's funeral.
7. It is no longer rung, but it is struck on special occasions.

Day 2—Other Symbols

Materials

- encyclopedias or other illustrated reference materials
- Symbol Sheet below

Activity

Have students write or dictate an explanation of each of these symbols of the United States.

Name _____   Date _____

Symbol Sheet

United States flag _____

_____

_____

_____

Statue of Liberty _____

_____

_____

_____

Uncle Sam _____

_____

_____

_____

Bald eagle _____

_____

_____

_____

Day 3—Design Your Own Symbol

Materials

- paper and art supplies

Activity

Ask students to design their own symbols for the United States and be ready to explain why they chose them and what they mean.

Day 4—Other Famous Bells

Materials

- encyclopedias or other illustrated reference materials

Activity

Have students find interesting facts about each of the following famous bells. Depending on the age group you are teaching, help students locate the information or have them use research materials on their own.

Big Ben in London

Church Bells of Dolores, Mexico

The King Bell in Russia

Day 5—I Wish.....

Materials

- writing materials, if desired

Activity

Have students finish this sentence in writing or orally: I wish I could hear the Liberty Bell ring because . . .

Background

Different resources give different dates for the invention and introduction of the bicycle. One of the dates mentioned is July 13, 1839. Since the bicycle is popular every day of the year, this date seems as good as any to learn about it.

Making It Work

Find out how many of your students ride bicycles. Some may still ride some kind of three-wheeler or use training wheels on their bikes, but safety rules are just as important for them as for more mature students—maybe more so.

Day 1—Bicycle Safety "Do's"

Materials

- See if you can get some primary safety materials from your local police department. They may even be willing to send an officer to talk about and demonstrate bicycle safety.

Activity

Ask your students to tell you about safe riding. Write their ideas on the board, shorten and synthesize them, and come up with a final version that can be lettered on poster board and left up in the classroom as a reminder. (See sample below.) Prepare copies and send them home with the pledge on page 85 so parents can reinforce the message.

Bicycle Safety "Do's" for Kids

1. Always wear a bike helmet.

2. Have someone check your bike for safe brakes and steering.

3. Use hand signals.

4. Walk your bike across intersections.

5. When you are old enough to ride in the street, use the bike lane if there is one.

6. Ride with the traffic, not against it.

Day 2—Bicycle Safety "Don'ts"

Materials

- see Day 1

Activity

Ask your students to tell you about unsafe riding. Write their ideas on the board, shorten and synthesize them, and come up with a final version that can be lettered on poster board and left up in the classroom as a reminder. (See sample below.)

Bicycle Safety "Don'ts" for Kids

1. Don't ride with two people on a one-person bike.

2. Don't do "wheelies" or other dangerous stunts.

3. Don't ride next to another bike rider. Ride single file.

4. Don't enter the street from between parked cars.

5. Don't carry things that block your view.

Day 3—Taking the Pledge

Materials

- a copy of the "Safety Pledge" (below) for each student

Activity

Give each student a copy of the "Safety Pledge." Read the pledge together as a class and discuss it. Ask students to take the pledge home along with the safety rules, and sign the pledge form with their parents.

I promise to obey all of the bicycle safety rules agreed to by my class.

Student's Signature _____

Parent's Signature _____

Day 4—Hand Signals

Materials

- hand signal picture (below) for each student

Activity

Pass out the hand signal pictures and have everyone lay them down on the desks.

Ask students to stand and practice the hand signals. Call out "left turn," "right turn," and "stop." Repeat the commands and mix them up. (Stand in the back of the room so you can observe the signals.)

Repeat this practice at intervals through the rest of the week and all year when you happen to think of it.

Day 5—I'm No Fool . . .

Materials

- *I'm No Fool on a Bicycle*, Disney safety film starring Jiminy Cricket

Activity

Show a safety film to culminate the week's emphasis on bicycle safety.

 Antarctica

Background

The continent of Antarctica was discovered on July 25, 1820, by Nathaniel B. Palmer, an American seal hunter.

Making It Work

Contact your school district's audiovisual department to see if you can obtain a film or video about Antarctica. The way penguins come out of the water onto the ice has to be seen to be believed!

Day 1—Cold Hard Facts

Materials

- encyclopedias or other illustrated reference materials
- classroom wall map of the world
- a globe

Activity

This is designed to be an oral exercise to establish a general base of information. See what the students already know and tell them the information they don't know. Go back and review for reinforcement.

- Antarctica is the third smallest continent. (Locate it on the map and the globe.)

- There are no countries at all on the continent.

- The South Pole is found in Antarctica.

- Antarctica contains one active volcano, Mount Erebus. (Locate it on the map.)

- The finger of land that reaches toward South America is the Antarctic Peninsula.

- There are many glaciers or slowly moving rivers of ice in Antarctica.

- Many seals live in the oceans around Antarctica; among them are the crabeater seal, the elephant seal, and the leopard seal.

- Many penguins live and nest around Antarctica. The emperor penguin is the largest; it can weigh up to 100 pounds (45 kg).

- Captain James Cook was the first explorer to sail around Antarctica.

- Roald Amundsen and Robert Scott were the first and second explorers to reach the South Pole.

Day 2—Penguin Poems

Materials

- encyclopedias or other illustrated reference materials
- an illustrated nonfiction book about penguins

Activity

Have students look at pictures of penguins, noticing what is unique about each type. For example, the emperor penguin looks as if he is wearing a tuxedo—a very well-dressed bird. The Adelie penguin courts his mate by presenting her with a specially selected pebble that he lays at her feet.

Have each student write and illustrate a short, humorous poem about one of these penguins. Share the poems as a large group and then display them on your creative writing bulletin board.

Day 3—Seal Stories

Materials

- encyclopedias or other illustrated reference materials
- research form below

Activity

Depending on the age group you are teaching, help students complete these statements or have them use research materials on their own.

Name _____   Date _____

Seal Stories

The elephant seal_____

_____.

The leopard seal_____

_____.

The crabeater seal _____

_____.

Day 4—The Cold Continent

Materials

- encyclopedias or other illustrated reference materials

Activity

Depending on the age group you are teaching, help students find the answers to these questions about Antarctica's climate or have them use research materials on their own.

1. Which place is colder, Antarctica or the Arctic?
2. What was the lowest temperature recorded in Antarctica?
3. Is the temperature colder along the coast or inland?
4. Why are scientists concerned about the effect of global warming on Antarctica?

Answers:

1. Antarctica is colder.
2. The lowest temperature was –127 degrees Fahrenheit (3 degrees Celsius), recorded at Vostok Station in August, 1960.
3. The temperature is colder inland.
4. The ice cap might melt and flood the rest of the world's coastal cities.

Day 5—Two Brave Men

Materials

- encyclopedias or other illustrated reference materials
- research form below

Activity

Depending on the age group you are teaching, help students complete these statements or have them use research materials on their own.

Two Brave Men

Roald Amundsen _____

_____.

Robert Scott _____

_____.

Background

The first week in August is National Clown Week. Becoming a clown is serious business. Many clowns learn their art in special schools. They are masters of pantomime, or acting without the use of words.

Making It Work

Invite a local clown to come to your classroom and demonstrate the application of makeup. Many clowns list themselves in the Yellow Pages to entertain at children's birthday parties. One of these clowns might put on a demonstration in exchange for sending home fliers. Check with your principal about making this kind of an arrangement.

Day 1—Plan a Clown Face

Materials

- paper and crayons
- circle patterns

Activity

Tell students that each clown designs his or her own face with makeup. No two clowns use the same face. Have each of them design a clown face by drawing a circle and experimenting with crayons. Save the design for the next activity.

Day 2—Make a Clown Mask

Materials

- large, thin white paper plates
- crayons or marking pens
- scissors
- cardboard egg cartons
- string or long wooden tongue depressors

Activity

Have students transfer their clown face designs to the backs of paper plates and color them. They can use sections cut from egg carton to fashion noses. Help students cut holes for eyes. Attach string if you want them to tie their masks on or fasten a tongue depressor to the bottom front so they can hold their masks up in front of their faces.

Day 3—What Do Clowns Do?

Materials

- encyclopedias or other illustrated reference materials

Activity

This is designed to be an oral exercise to establish a general base of information. See what the students already know and give them the information they don't have. Expand on and discuss the different ideas for reinforcement.

- Clowns provide comic relief between dramatic and dangerous performances in the circus. After watching people perform on the flying trapeze, for example, the audience can relax by watching the clowns.

- Since circus acts are performed in an open space, there is no way to bring down the curtain between acts. Clowns fill in the time and distract people while one set of performers leave and another act enters.

- Clowns perform an even more important and dangerous function in rodeos and western shows. They distract the animals so riders who have been thrown off can get out of the ring or arena without being trampled.

- Clowns can be enjoyed just for their own acts, as well as for the other functions they perform. Many of them are expert jugglers as well as tightrope performers and bareback riders.

- A clown's costume and makeup are a personal trademark. No one else can dress or use makeup in exactly the same way.

- Emmett Kelly was a famous American clown, known for his impersonation of a sad-faced tramp.

- The Keystone Cops were famous American clowns, too. Their most famous act involved many people getting out of a tiny car. They appeared in a series of early movies.

- Clowns are important in European countries, too. They use a makeup style known as whiteface.

- All clowns use a kind of heavy theatrical makeup called grease paint.

Day 4—Clown Cupcakes

Materials

- plain baked cupcakes
- frosting in assorted colors
- cake decorations such as sprinkles, spicy cinnamon drops, and licorice whips

Activity

Have fun decorating cupcakes to look like clown faces. Divide the class into groups and put small bowls of frosting on the tables. Let each student create his or her own clown-face cupcake. Put them aside for Friday's refreshments.

Day 5—Circus Posters

Materials

- poster board or large sheets of drawing paper
- crayons or markers
- scratch paper and pencils

Activity

Have student groups meet to plan and create a circus poster advertising a clown act. Display the finished posters around the classroom and enjoy the cupcakes you made yesterday.

Background

Davy Crockett was born on August 17, 1786. He was a scout, an army officer, and a congressman from Tennessee for three terms. He died at the Alamo where his diary was found when the ruins were searched.

Making It Work

Davy Crockett is one of those people who symbolizes American frontier days. Although he was a real person, he is most famous for the tall tales told about his life in the backwoods. He told most of the tall tales himself and wrote three books about his adventures. He has achieved the kind of legendary status shared by Pecos Bill, Paul Bunyan, Mike Fink, and John Henry.

Day 1—King of the Wild Frontier

Materials

- encyclopedias or other illustrated reference materials
- classroom wall map of the United States

Activity

This is designed to be an oral exercise to establish a general base of information. See what the students already know and give them the information they don't have. Locate places on the map as you go along.

- Davy Crockett was born in Tennessee on August 17, 1786.
- He was a scout, an army officer, an Indian fighter, and a congressman from Tennessee for three terms.
- Even though he had many real accomplishments, he is best known for the tall tales told about his adventures on the frontier. He told most of these tall tales himself and even wrote three books about his adventures.
- He died in 1836 defending the Alamo in Texas. His diary was found in the ruins.
- He has been the subject of movies and TV shows, and songs have been written about his life and adventures. He has become part of American folklore.

Day 2—What Is Folklore?

Materials

- encyclopedias or other illustrated reference materials

Activity

Depending on the age group you are teaching, help students answer these questions about folklore or have them use research materials on their own.

Name _____ Date _____

1. What is folklore? _____

   _____

2. What is a myth? _____

   _____

3. What is a fable? _____

   _____

4. What is a legend? _____

   _____

5. What is a fairy tale? _____

   _____

6. Are there other kinds of folklore? _____

   _____

7. What is different about American folklore? _____

   _____

Answers:

1. In general, it is all of the stories that are passed from one generation to another without being written down.
2. A myth is a kind of folklore that explains life and death and the great forces of nature.
3. A fable is a kind of folklore that teaches people how to live by telling stories about animals and stating a moral at the end.
4. A legend also teaches, but it is closer to real life and may be partly true.
5. A fairy tale is a magical story told to entertain.
6. There are songs, proverbs, Mother Goose rhymes, and so on.
7. Since American folk customs started after the invention of printing, all of American folklore has been written down. Many of the stories are legends and tall tales.

Day 3—Paul Bunyan and Babe

Materials

- A book of American folktales, including stories of Paul Bunyan and his blue ox, Babe— An excellent resource is *American Tall Tales* by Mary Pope Osborne (Alfred A. Knopf, 1991).

Activity

Read aloud to your class several Paul Bunyan stories.

Discuss tall tales.

Day 4—The Legend of Sleepy Hollow

Materials

- book and/or Disney video of *The Legend of Sleepy Hollow*

Activity

There are several primary level editions of Washington Irving's book. Two resources are *Legend of Sleepy Hollow* by Patricia A. Jensen (First-Start Tall Tale Series., Troll, 1995) and *Legend of Sleepy Hollow* by Jan Gleiter (Raintree Steck-Vaughn, 1993. (The Disney video is a retelling based on the story of the same name as recorded by Washington Irving in *The Sketch Book*, a collection of folklore from the Eastern part of the U.S.)

Discuss humorous and regional folktales.

Day 5—Pocahontas

Materials

- book and/ or Disney video of *Pocahontas*

Activity

Read a book and/or show *Pocahontas* to your class. There are several books published about Pocahontas. One good resource is Ingri d'Aulaire's *Pocahontas* (Doubleday, 1989).

Discuss legends—stories based on facts and real people from American history.

Background

On August 21, 1959, Hawaii became the 50th state of the union. Another star was added to the flag, giving it the appearance it has today.

Making It Work

Find out if any of your students have been to Hawaii (unless, of course, you live there!) Ask these students to share their impressions and experiences.

Day 1—Tropical Trivia

Materials

- encyclopedias or other illustrated reference materials
- travel brochures from a travel agency

Activity

This is designed to be an oral exercise to establish a general base of information. See what the students already know and give them the information they don't have. Expand on and discuss the different ideas for reinforcement.

- On August 21, 1959, Hawaii became the 50th state of the union. Another star was added to the flag, making it look the way it does today.

- The Hawaiian Islands are the tops of volcanoes that have pushed their way up from the bottom of the Pacific Ocean. Some of these volcanoes are still active.

- The Hawaiian Island group consists of more than 20 islands, reefs, and atolls stretching across more than 1,900 miles (3,040 km) of the Pacific Ocean. Only the eight largest islands make up the state of Hawaii. They are Hawaii, Kahoolawe, Kaui, Lanai, Maui, Molokai, Niihau, and Oahu. No one lives on Kahoolawe, and Niihau is privately owned.

- Honolulu, on the island of Oahu, is the capital of Hawaii.

- The state flower is the hibiscus, the state tree is the kukui, and the state bird is the nene, the Hawaiian goose.

- Hawaii is called the "Aloha State." "Aloha" is the Hawaiian word for "greetings."

- Hawaiians wear leis or garlands of flowers on happy occasions. Leis are often presented to travelers when they arrive in Hawaii.

Day 2—Hawaiian Geography

Materials

- an atlas or encyclopedia with a political map of Hawaii showing the eight islands
- a classroom wall map of the world
- copies of the outline map below

Activity

Locate the Hawaiian Islands on the world map. Then, on the outline map, label each island with its name and mark the location of Honolulu on the island of Oahu.

The Hawaiian Islands

Pacific Ocean

Day 3—Hawaiian History

Materials

- encyclopedias or other illustrated reference materials

Activity

Depending on the age group you are teaching, help students find the answers to these questions about the history of Hawaii or have them use research materials on their own.

1. Who discovered Hawaii? In what year?
2. What did he call the islands? Why?
3. Who ruled the islands at that time?
4. How did the islands become a monarchy and how long did it last?
5. When did Hawaii become a territory of the United States?

> **Answers:** 1. Captain James Cook of the British Navy in 1778; 2. the Sandwich Islands, in honor of the Earl of Sandwich; 3. a number of tribal chieftains; 4. A strong chieftain united the islands as a monarchy which lasted until 1893.; 5. in 1900

Day 4—Plan-a-Trip Day

Materials

- encyclopedias or other illustrated reference materials
- travel brochures from a travel agency

Activity

Have students meet in groups to plan a trip to Hawaii. Where would they go? What would they see and do? Let groups share plans.

Day 5—Make-a-Lei Day

Materials

- necklace-length pieces of string
- blunt craft needles
- crepe or tissue paper

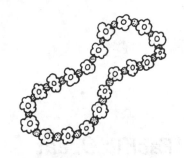

Activity

Cut circles of crepe or tissue paper and string them, pushing them tight on the string to make them look like hibiscus flowers. Tie and wear around your neck.

Background

On August 24, 79 A.D., Mount Vesuvius erupted, burying the cities of Herculaneum, Pompeii, and Stabiae with lava and ashes. An eyewitness account of this eruption has come down to us from Pliny the Younger.

Making It Work

This eruption was so sudden that a picture of life as it was lived in 79 A.D. has been preserved for us to see. Many archaeologists have made a study of this area their lives' work.

Day 1—A Picture of History

Materials

- encyclopedias or other illustrated reference materials
- classroom wall map of the world

Activity

This is designed to be an oral exercise to establish a general base of information. See what the students already know and give them the information they don't have. Help students locate Italy on the world map.

- On August 24, 79 A.D., Mount Vesuvius erupted, burying the cities of Herculaneum, Pompeii, and Stabiae under tons of lava and ashes.

- People knew about this event because a man named Pliny the Younger saw the eruption and wrote a letter describing it, but the location of the cities was lost for hundreds of years.

- More than half of the city of Pompeii has now been excavated. Tourists can walk through the same streets and buildings that people used almost 2,000 years ago.

- The ruins of Herculaneum were buried much deeper than those of Pompeii and were not discovered until the early 1700s.

- The area is honeycombed with tunnels dug by robbers, and it is believed that many priceless treasures have been carried off.

- Thousands of items recovered from the ruins of both Pompeii and Herculaneum are on display in the National Museum at Naples, which is about 13 miles away.

Day 2—Inside a Volcano

Materials

- encyclopedias or other illustrated reference materials
- copies of the volcano diagram below

Activity

Depending on the age group you are teaching, help students label the parts of the volcano shown on the diagram or have them use research materials on their own.

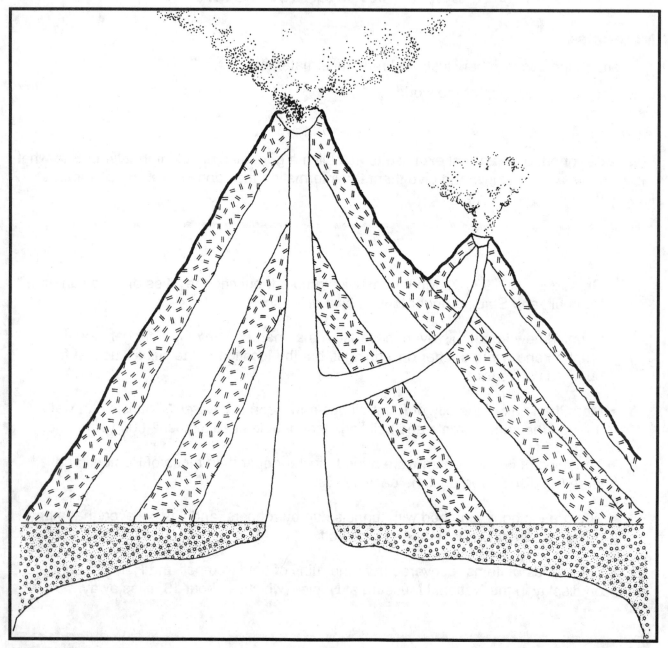

Day 3—Other Volcanoes

Materials

- a film or video showing volcanic eruptions (There are good ones of Hawaiian volcanoes.)

Activity

Show students a film or video of erupting volcanoes. Tell them that most of the footage available is of the Hawaiian volcanoes. Scientists have always felt safe studying and filming the Hawaiian volcanoes until recently, when there have been more violent and destructive eruptions. Discuss the film.

Day 4—More Volcanoes

Materials

- encyclopedias or other illustrated reference materials
- paper and pencil

Activity

Depending on the age group you are teaching, help students locate the following information or have them use research materials on their own.

Find out at least one fact about each volcano listed below. Write the facts on paper.

Diamond Head	Mount Fuji
Kilimanjaro	Popocatepetl
Krakatoa	Mount Saint Helens

Day 5—Make a Volcano

Materials

- dirt
- vinegar
- red food coloring
- water
- baking soda
- small glass jar
- liquid dish washing detergent
- tablespoon
- measuring cup

Activity

Make a hill out of dirt and bury the jar in the top with the mouth exposed for the crater. Put 5 tablespoons of baking soda in the jar. Mix 1 cup (250 mL) of water, $1/2$ cup (125 mL) dish washing liquid, and $1/2$ cup (125 mL) vinegar in another container. Add food coloring. Pour some in the jar. "Lava" should bubble up and pour down the sides.

Background

Labor Day is celebrated on the first Monday in September. It is traditionally thought of as the last weekend of summer and is one of the original three-day weekends. The holiday was instituted to honor American workers. President Grover Cleveland signed a bill making Labor Day a legal holiday in 1894.

Making It Work

If you teach in a school with a traditional school year, Labor Day may be over when school begins. You can celebrate it after the fact, however, as a happy look at the summer that has just ended. It is also a great time to start a unit on careers.

Day 1—Working Facts

Materials

- encyclopedias or other illustrated reference materials

Activity

This is designed to be an oral exercise to establish a general base of information. See what the students already know and give them the information they don't have.

- Labor Day is celebrated on the first Monday in September. It is a day set aside to honor American workers.

- Labor Day grew out of the labor movement to obtain better pay for workers and establish safe working conditions.

- The Knights of Labor held the first Labor Day Parade in New York City in 1882.

- Oregon was the first state to recognize Labor Day in 1887.

- President Grover Cleveland signed a bill making it a legal holiday in 1894.

- Labor Day is traditionally thought of as the last weekend of summer and is one of the original three-day weekends.

- Many people celebrate the Labor Day weekend with a last trip to the beach or lake, a visit to an amusement park, or a big family picnic or barbecue.

Day 2—What Do You Want to Be?

Materials

- encyclopedias or other illustrated reference materials   • writing materials

Activity

Have students write (or dictate to you or an instructional assistant) a paragraph about what they want to be when they grow up. Share completed work with the whole class and discuss.

Day 3—What Do You Want to Be? _(cont.)_

Materials

- a large piece of paper or poster board
- small squares cut out of construction paper to fit the size of the graph you will make
- glue sticks

Activity

Write "Career Graph" across the top of the paper or poster board. Go through the student's "What I Want to Be" papers and write the various career titles at intervals across the bottom. Give students squares of construction paper and have them affix their squares of paper, making a vertical column above the appropriate career title.

Career Graph

| Doctor | Astronaut | Teacher | Lawyer | Engineer |

Day 4—What Do You Want to Be? *(cont.)*

Materials

- drawing paper
- art materials
- "What I Want to Be" paragraphs

Activity

Have each student draw a picture representing the career he or she chose. They can draw symbols such as a stethoscope for a doctor or a rocket for an astronaut or a wrench for a plumber.

Mount their "What I Want to Be" paragraphs on the backs of the career pictures.

Arrange with another teacher to let your class bring its Labor Day Parade to his or her classroom. Students can parade in, display their pictures, and read their paragraphs one at a time.

Day 5—Labor Day Picnic

Materials

- sack lunches or prepared school lunches
- a few playground balls and/or jump ropes

Activity

Have a Labor Day picnic with lunch on the grass or at lunch tables where you can have your whole class together.

- Arrange to stay out on the playground after the end-of-lunch bell rings to make the occasion special.
- Play a few games such as relay races or jump rope contests.
- Let everybody have some time to talk about his or her summer experiences.

Background

Grandparent's Day is the second Sunday in September. It is a fairly new holiday, but it is gaining recognition. There are more older people now than there used to be because life expectancy is increasing. More older people appear in commercials because advertisers are trying to appeal to that age group. Extended families are more common than they were for awhile because people once again are realizing that the generations can help one another.

Making It Work

Find out how many children in your class have grandparents who are living nearby. Perhaps some grandparents could be coaxed to come into the classroom to help by listening to children read or by reading to them.

Day 1—Special Stories

Materials

- writing materials
- construction paper
- markers or crayons

Activity

Help students compose special stories for their grandparents with starters such as, "My grandmother (or grandfather) is special because . . ."

The following are some ideas to get students started:

- He plays games with me.
- She makes cookies for me.
- He reads to me.
- She always has time to talk.

If students do not have grandparents, perhaps they can write to another older relative, neighbor, or friend. (Remember to be sensitive to the needs of students who may have recently lost grandparents; perhaps they can write biographies commemorating their relatives.)

After stories are completed, help students to edit and recopy them on good quality paper. The stories can then be mounted on a half sheet of construction paper and decorated with a border.

Day 2—Coupon Books

Materials

- paper
- writing materials
- art supplies

Day 2—Coupon Books *(cont.)*

Activity

Have students make and illustrate personalized coupons that can be stapled into book form like those suggested for Mother's Day and Father's Day. Children can include coupons for things that would be particularly meaningful to their grandparents.

Happy Grandparent's Day	**Good for** _____ _____ _____ _____ _____ _____

Day 3—Adopt a Senior Citizen

Materials

- writing materials
- construction paper
- markers or crayons

Activity

Find a retirement home or senior center whose clients would welcome cards from your students. If the facility is close by, perhaps your class could take a walking field trip to present the cards. Otherwise, you can collect them from the students and mail them all together.

Tell students that many older people do not have families close by and that they may appreciate receiving cards.

Give students some ideas to get them started:

- Draw a happy sun on the front of a card. On the inside, write: I hope your day is full of sunshine!
- Draw a rainbow on the front of the card. On the inside, write: May your wishes come true!

Day 4—Adopt a Senior Citizen *(cont.)*

Materials

- writing materials

Activity

If you contact a senior center rather than a nursing home, find out if anyone there would like to come to school once a week and either read to the children or listen to them read. Have the students write letters of invitation to any likely prospects.

Help students edit and recopy their letters. You may want to follow up with a phone call. You may also need to help arrange for transportation to the school.

Day 5—My Family Tree

Materials

- writing materials

- Family Tree form below

Activity

Explain the idea of a family tree to students. Have them take home the form and ask their parents to show them where their grandparents fit on the family tree.

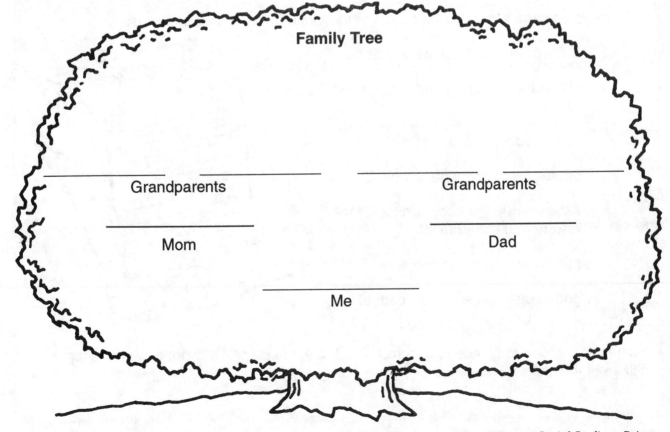

Family Tree

Grandparents   Grandparents

Mom   Dad

Me

Background

September 17 was once called "Constitution Day" because the Constitution was signed on that date. It later became "I Am an American Day." Today, it is called "Citizenship Day" because it is the day naturalization ceremonies are held.

Making It Work

Ask your students if they have a family member who has become a naturalized citizen. Perhaps that person would come to school and describe the process to your class.

Day 1—The Facts

Materials

- encyclopedias or other illustrated reference materials

Activity

This is designed to be an oral exercise to establish a general base of information. See what the students already know and give them the information they don't have. Expand on and discuss different ideas for reinforcement.

In order to become a naturalized citizen of the United States a person must . . .

> . . . file a petition to become a citizen.

> . . . live in the United States continuously for five years.

> . . . have good moral character.

> . . . speak, read, and write simple English.

> . . . have knowledge about United States history and government.

> . . . pass a test on these subjects.

> . . . go to court and swear an oath of allegiance.

People study for a long time to accomplish all of these steps. It is not easy to become a citizen of the United States.

Day 2—Good Citizens Obey the Laws

Materials

- paper and pencils
- crayons or markers

Activity

Have a discussion with your class about laws.

- What are laws?
  (rules people agree to live by)

- Which laws affect students?
  (laws about traffic and safety, school attendance, stealing, etc.)

Have students draw a picture showing a student obeying a law. Collect the pictures and save them for Friday.

Day 3—Good Citizens Vote

Materials

- paper and pencils
- crayons or markers

Activity

Have a discussion with your class about voting.

- What is voting?
  (saying what you want by casting a ballot)

- Who can vote?
  (all citizens age eighteen and over)

- Why is it important for people to vote?
  (answers will vary)

Have students draw a picture showing people voting. Collect the pictures and save them for Friday.

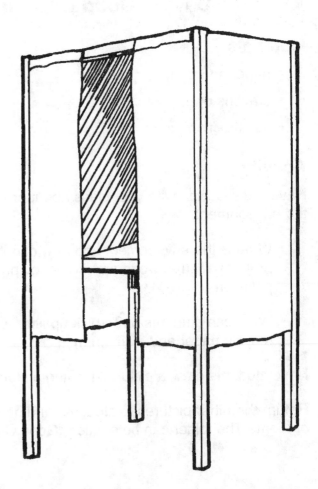

Day 4—Good Citizens Help Other People

Materials

- paper and pencils
- crayons or markers

Activity

Have a discussion with your class about helping others.

- What does it mean to help others?
  (answers will vary)

- How can students help others?
  (many ways: call 911 in an emergency, for example)

Have students draw a picture showing a student helping someone. Collect the pictures and save them for Friday.

Day 5—Good Citizens Protect the Environment

Materials

- paper and pencils
- crayons or markers
- construction paper

Activity

Have a discussion with your class about protecting the environment.

- What is the environment and how can it be protected? (the world around us; by preventing pollution)

- What can students do? (pick up litter, save and recycle paper and aluminum)

Have students draw a picture showing a student doing something to protect the environment.

Return the other pictures to students and have them make a construction paper folder for all of them. The folder can be entitled "Good Citizens."

Background

Johnny Appleseed's real name was John Chapman. He was born in 1774, in Leominster, Massachusetts, and died in 1845 near Fort Wayne, Indiana. No one knows where he was buried, but monuments have been built in his honor in several places. He was a very religious person and felt that planting apple trees was his mission in life.

Making It Work

Review with students what they already learned about folklore when they did the activity for Davy Crockett. The legend of Johnny Appleseed is a perfect example of American folklore because he was a real person whose story grew until it became bigger than life.

Day 1—The Legend

Materials

- a film or video about Johnny Appleseed (A great one was made by Disney and featured the voice of Dennis Day. You may be able to find it in your school district's audiovisual department.)

- a book about Johnny Appleseed (A good book is *Johnny Appleseed* by Steven Kellogg, Morrow, 1988.)

Activity

Show the film or read the book aloud to your class. Discuss the elements that make the story a legend rather than history.

Have students write (or dictate to you or an instructional assistant) the story of Johnny Appleseed.

When the stories are finished, have each student read his or her story to the class. Did they stick to the story as it was presented? Did they change anything? Add anything?

If any students did change or add anything, you can discuss it as an example of how legends grow as they are retold.

Have students recopy and illustrate their stories. Display them on a bulletin board titled, "Our Legends of Johnny Appleseed."

Day 2—The Facts

Materials

- encyclopedias or other illustrated reference materials

Activity

This is designed to be an oral exercise to establish a general base of information. See what the students already know and give them the information they don't have. Expand on and discuss the different ideas for reinforcement.

- Johnny Appleseed's real name was John Chapman.

- He was born on September 26, 1774.

- He cleared the land and planted apple trees for the settlers he knew would be coming soon.

- He traveled through Ohio and Indiana, where he died in March, 1845, near Fort Wayne.

- No one knows where he was buried, but monuments have been built in his honor in several places.

- He was a very religious person and felt that planting apple trees was his mission in life.

Day 3—All about Apples

Materials

- encyclopedias or other illustrated reference materials
- *The Life and Times of the Apple* by Charles Micucci (Orchard Books, 1992)

Activity

Read *The Life and Times of the Apple* aloud to your class. Discuss the information in the book in addition to the topics listed below.

- Apples are grown more widely than any other fruit.

- They grow everywhere in the world except the very hottest and coldest regions.

- The apple was brought to America by the earliest European settlers, but people think of it now as a typically American fruit. We even have a saying that something can be "as American as apple pie."

- Today the United States is one of the world's leading producers of apples.

Day 4—Kinds of Apples

Materials

- encyclopedias or other illustrated reference materials

Activity

Depending on the age group you are teaching, help students find information about apples or have them use research materials on their own.

Name _____ Date _____

Write at least one fact about each of these kinds of apples:

- Delicious _____
- Macintosh _____
- Winesap _____
- Rome Beauty _____
- Gravenstein _____
- Jonathan _____
- Granny Smith _____

Day 5—Apple Games

Materials

- apples

Activity

Pioneers, who had no electricity and few toys to play with, amused themselves with apple games like these.

Pass the Apple: Students stand in a line, shoulder to shoulder. Tuck an apple under the chin of the first student. The object of the game is to pass the apple down the line without using the hands. Two teams can compete.

Apple Push: Students race, pushing apples across the floor with their noses.

Hanging Apple: Hang an apple from the ceiling with a long string tied to its stem. Students try to grab it, using only their teeth.

Finish up by eating apples!

Background

The fourth Friday in September is celebrated as Native American Day in some states, especially those with large Native American populations. Although this day is not recognized by the Bureau of Indian Affairs, it is becoming more and more well known around the country. It is a good time to motivate interest in the Native Americans and dispel some of the stereotypes that have developed.

Making It Work

Talk about the way ideas have changed in regard to Native Americans. Not too long ago people spoke of Indians and thought of them as the "bad guys" in a Western movie. Now, people realize that Native Americans were subjected to unfair treatment when European settlers came in and took their lands.

Day 1—In Harmony with Nature

Materials

- encyclopedias or other illustrated reference materials
- *Buffalo Hunt* by Russell Freedman, Holiday House, 1988
- *Keepers of the Earth: Native American Stories and Environment Activities for Children* by Michael J. Caduto and Joseph Bruchau, Fulcrum, 1988 (This is a wonderful resource book for teachers.)

Activity

Read *Buffalo Hunt* aloud to your class. Discuss the following topics:

> **ways in which the Native Americans hunted the buffalo**

> **ways in which they used the buffalo for food, clothing, housing, tools**

Day 2—Native Americans of the Northeast

Materials

- encyclopedias or other illustrated reference materials

Activity

Depending on the age group you are teaching, help students find information about Native Americans of the Northeast or have them use research materials on their own.

Name _____ Date _____

Native Americans of the Northeast

Territory_____

Type of Shelter _____

Transportation_____

Other Facts_____

Day 3—Native Americans of the Plains

Materials

- encyclopedias or other illustrated reference materials

Activity

Depending on the age group you are teaching, help students find information about Native Americans of the Plains or have them use research materials on their own.

Name _____ Date _____

Native Americans of the Plains

Territory_____

Type of Shelter _____

Transportation_____

Other Facts_____

Day 4—Native Americans of the Northwest

Materials

- encyclopedias or other illustrated reference materials

Activity

Depending on the age group you are teaching, help students find information about Native Americans of the Northwest or have them use research materials on their own.

Name _____ Date _____

Native Americans of the Northwest

Territory_____

Type of Shelter _____

Transportation_____

Other Facts_____

Day 5—Native Americans of the Southwest

Materials

- encyclopedias or other illustrated reference materials

Activity

Depending on the age group you are teaching, help students find information about Native Americans of the Southwest or have them use research materials on their own.

Name _____ Date _____

Native Americans of the Southwest

Territory_____

Type of Shelter _____

Transportation_____

Other Facts_____

Background

Each year the President of the United States sets aside a week in early October as Fire Prevention Week. Fires cause thousands of deaths and billions of dollars in property damage in the U.S. every year. It is more important to teach people how to prevent fires than to develop new and better ways of putting them out.

Making It Work

The week when fire departments and the media are publicizing fire prevention is a good time to start your own fire prevention program. Arrange to take your students on a field trip to a nearby fire station, if possible, as many of them will have an open house this week. Make sure your school has a fire drill this week, also.

Day 1—Fire Facts

Materials

- encyclopedias or other illustrated reference materials

Activity

This is designed to be an oral exercise to establish a general base of information. See what the students already know and give them the information they don't have. Expand on and discuss the different ideas for reinforcement.

Controlled fire is one of humanity's best friends. Primitive people used fire for:

- heating
- cooking
- turning clay into pottery
- light

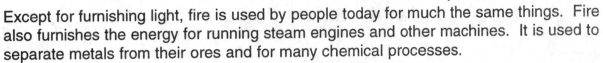

Except for furnishing light, fire is used by people today for much the same things. Fire also furnishes the energy for running steam engines and other machines. It is used to separate metals from their ores and for many chemical processes.

Uncontrolled fire is one of humanity's worst enemies.

Fires have caused many deaths and billions of dollars in property damage in the United States.

Some fires are brought about by natural causes. Lightning often starts forest fires.

Some fires are caused by carelessness, and others are set on purpose.

Day 2—Safety Walk

Materials

- a map of the school for each student

Activity

Take a walk around your school and note the position of fire alarm boxes, fire extinguishers, fire hydrants, or the forest fire station. Have students mark all of these on their maps.

When you get back to the classroom, pool all of your information and make one good copy of the map. Run off enough copies to give to the school office and each classroom in the school to post for their information and safety.

Give some consideration to discussing the serious offense of giving a false alarm. Most schools have very severe penalties for this kind of misbehavior, and students should be warned ahead of time of the consequences for pulling such a prank.

Day 3—Safety Plan

Materials

- writing materials

Activity

Have students draw a sketch of the floor plan of their homes, indicating doors and windows and a second story if they have one. If they live in an apartment or condominium, have them show stairways and attached buildings.

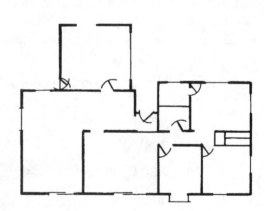

Send these sketches home with your students so they can discuss it with their parents and make family plans for escaping from a fire.

Day 4—Safety Posters

Materials

- large paper or poster board
- art materials

Activity

Have students create posters for Fire Prevention Week. Remind them to think of a good slogan and to use simple, bright pictures and big letters. Put the posters up around the school.

Day 5—Fire Fighting Equipment

Materials

- copies of the illustrations below

Activity

Find out about and discuss each kind of fire engine.

Pumper

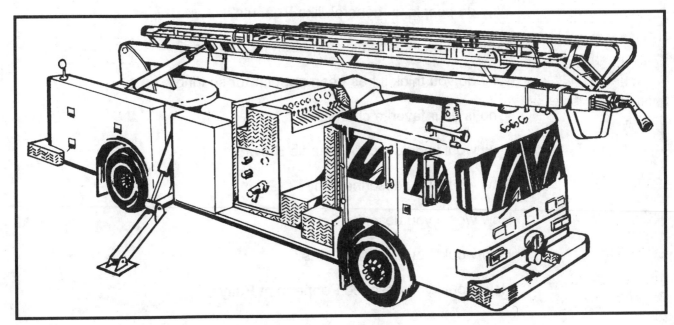

Ladder Truck

Background

On October 3, 1950, the first "Peanuts" comic strip was published. It was created by Charles M. Schulz.

Making It Work

Gather together as many collections of Peanuts cartoons as you can obtain. Have them available in the classroom for leisure reading. Clip some current "Peanuts" comic strips from the newspaper and make a "Peanuts" bulletin board.

Day 1—Read Around

Materials

- a collection of *Peanuts* books

Activity

Tell students that the first "Peanuts" comic strip was published on October 3, 1950. Distribute books to partners or individual students, depending on how many books you were able to gather. Give students time to read and share their favorites. Discuss the answers to the following questions.

Why do you like Peanuts?

Why do people, in general, like Peanuts?

How long has the comic strip been in existence?

Why do you think it has been popular for so long?

Who is your favorite character?

How would you describe Charlie Brown?

How would you describe Lucy?

How would you describe Snoopy?

How would you describe Linus?

How would you describe Peppermint Patty?

Day 2—On Film

Materials

- a "Peanuts" video (*A Charlie Brown Christmas* will probably be the easiest to find.)

Activity

Show the film to your class.

Then, discuss and compare the characters on film to the characters in the comic strip.

Which do you like better?

Do their voices sound the way you thought they would?

Do they move the way you had imagined them moving?

Day 3—Drawing a Cartoon Character

Materials

- paper and pencils
- fine-line black markers
- art gum erasers or other big, soft eraser

Activity

Tell students that the definition of a comic strip is a series of drawings that tell a story quickly. Have each student experiment with developing a comic strip character. The drawing can be as simple as a stick figure with a round head.

Tell students to draw lightly with their pencils, as they will be erasing the lines later.

Have students try to draw their characters in different positions—standing, sitting, running, turning sideways.

Have students add clothing to their figures.

Have students experiment with adding ears and hair to a round face and then drawing different expressions.

Show students how to carefully ink in the lines they want to keep with black marking pen. Let the drawing dry and then erase the pencil lines.

Day 4—Drawing Charlie Brown

Materials

- paper and pencils
- tracing paper

Activity

Have students practice drawing or tracing some of the Charlie Brown characters. They can then use them to make their own "Pretend Peanuts" four-panel comic strips, using their own words in the dialogue balloons.

Have students display and share their completed comic strips.

Day 5—Original Comic Strips

Materials

- cartoon characters created on Day 3

Activity

Encourage students to turn their original character(s) into a four-panel comic strip.

122

Background

On October 12, 1492, Columbus sighted the island of San Salvador off the east coast of Central America. Thinking he had reached the East Indies, he called the native inhabitants Indians.

Making It Work

It is interesting for the students to note that Columbus did not set out to prove the world was round. He assumed that everyone knew this to be a fact, as did most educated people of his time. Columbus set out to reach the East by sailing west in order to find a short sea route to the Indies. His error lay in underestimating the size of Earth and in not knowing that America was in the way of his course.

Day 1—What Really Happened

Materials

- encyclopedias or other illustrated reference materials

Activity

This is designed to be an oral exercise to establish a general base of information. See what the students already know and give them the information they don't have. Expand on and discuss the different ideas for reinforcement.

- Columbus was born in 1451 in Genoa, Italy.

- He was the eldest of five children and as a youth had always longed to go to sea.

- As a young man, he shipped out on several voyages, at least one of which nearly cost him his life.

- By 1477, he had learned that the Portuguese were trying to reach the Indies by sailing east around the continent of Africa.

- To the king of Portugal, he tried to sell his plan for reaching the Indies by sailing west. The king refused to sponsor Columbus.

- Columbus gained the favor of Queen Isabella of Spain, who financed his voyage. She offered to pawn the crown jewels to help him, but the royal treasurer managed to come up with the money instead.

- Columbus discovered the New World when he sighted San Salvador on October 12, 1492. He returned in triumph to Spain in 1493.

- Columbus made three more voyages to the New World. He always believed that San Salvador was one of the islands of the East Indies near Japan or China.

Day 2—Columbus, the Man

Materials

- encyclopedia or other illustrated reference materials

Activity

Depending on the age group you are teaching, help students find information about Columbus or have them use research materials on their own.

Name _____ Date _____

1. What did Columbus look like? _____

   _____

2. How did he dress? _____

   _____

3. How did he act? _____

   _____

4. What did he think was his mission in life? _____

   _____

- -

Answers:

1. He was tall and well built with a long face and thin nose. His hair was blonde but turned white when he was 30.
2. He was simple in his dress.
3. He was pleasant but dignified and ate and drank moderately.
4. He believed God wanted him to make great discoveries in order to spread Christianity.

Day 3—In My Opinion

Materials

- writing materials

Activity

Have students write (or dictate to you or to an instructional assistant) their opinion of Columbus. They can begin, "In my opinion, Columbus was . . ." or, "I think Columbus . . ." When they are finished, have students share and compare their opinions. Discuss differences. Ask them to give reasons for their opinions.

Day 4—Columbus' Ships

Materials

- encyclopedias or other illustrated reference materials

Activity

Depending on the age group you are teaching, help students find information about Columbus' ships or have them use research materials on their own.

Name _____ Date _____

1. How many ships did Columbus have on his first voyage? _____

2. How long was the *Santa Maria*, Columbus' flagship? _____

3. How many men made up the crew of the *Santa Maria*? _____

4. What were the names of the other two ships? _____

5. What were the ships made of? _____

6. How long did it take Columbus' ships to cross the Atlantic Ocean? _____

7. How long does it take a modern ship to cross the Atlantic Ocean? _____

Answers: 1. three ships; 2. about 90 feet (27 meters) long; 3. 40 men; 4.the *Niña* and the *Pinta;* 5. wood; 6. 36 days; 7. Some take less than 5 days.

Day 5—Sea Serpents

Materials

- encyclopedias or other illustrated reference materials

Activity

Tell your students that most experts today say that Columbus' crews were not worried about sea serpents. They were more concerned about the strong winds that blew from the east. However, many people in the 1400s did believe in sea serpents; some people still believe in them today. And some huge animals do live in the sea. Have students find out something about each of these sea creatures: basking shark, oarfish, giant squid. Then have students write something about each and draw a picture showing their ideas of a sea serpent.

Background

On October 14, 1744, the Earl of Sandwich put a piece of meat between two slices of bread and created the world's first sandwich.

Making It Work

The Earl of Sandwich may not be as historically important as Columbus, but he certainly had an effect on our everyday lives. Have fun with sandwiches this week. On Day 2 through Day 5, you can either make the "sandwiches" or just talk about them.

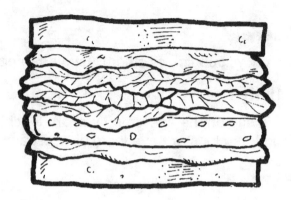

Day 1—Fun Facts

Materials

- encyclopedias or other illustrated reference materials

Activity

This is designed to be an oral exercise to establish a general base of information. See what the students already know and give them the information they don't have. Expand on and discuss the different ideas for reinforcement.

- On October 14, 1744, the Earl of Sandwich created the kind of food that is still called by his name.

- The story goes that he was playing cards and did not want to stop to eat, so he asked for two slices of bread with a piece of meat between them.

- The sandwich has come a long way since 1744, as there are plain sandwiches and fancy sandwiches, hot sandwiches and cold sandwiches, and even sandwiches named after cartoon characters. The "Whimpy" is a hamburger named after a character in Popeye. The "Dagwood" is a sandwich piled with all kinds of ingredients and named after Dagwood in "Blondie and Dagwood."

- People in Sweden make small, open-faced sandwiches by arranging the ingredients so they look like little pictures or designs.

Day 2—U.S.A.: Bologna or Peanut Butter and Jelly

Materials

sandwich makings, if desired:

- bread
- peanut butter and jelly

    or

- bologna and mayonnaise

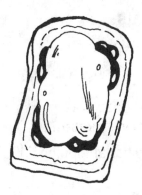

Activity

Ask students how to make either a peanut butter or a bologna sandwich. Write the steps on the board as you go.

What is the first step? (Lay out the bread.)

What is the second step? (Spread peanut butter or mayonnaise on the bread.)

What is the third step? (Add jelly or bologna.)

What is the fourth step? (Top with second slice of bread.)

What is the fifth step? (Eat the sandwich.)

Day 3—Mexico: Burrito

Materials

burrito makings:

- soft flour tortilla
- refried beans
- grated cheese

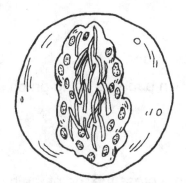

Activity

Ask students how to make a burrito. Write the steps on the board as you go.

What is the first step? (Lay out the tortilla.)

What is the second step? (Spread beans down the middle of the tortilla.)

What is the third step? (Cover the beans with grated cheese.)

What is the fourth step? (Fold up one end of the tortilla and roll the sides over.)

What is the fifth step? (Eat the burrito.)

Day 4—Italy: Pizza

Materials

pizza makings:

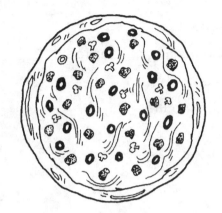

- pizza dough (use pre-baked pizza shell)

- tomato sauce

- grated cheese

- additional toppings, if desired

Activity

Ask students how to make a pizza. Write the steps on the board as you go.

What is the first step? (Lay out the dough.)

What is the second step? (Spread sauce over the dough.)

What is the third step? (Add toppings, such as pepperoni.)

What is the fourth step? (Cover the whole top with grated cheese.)

What is the fifth step? (Bake or heat the pizza.)

What is the sixth step? (Eat the pizza.)

Day 5—Favorite Sandwich Graph

Material

- large piece of paper or poster board

- small squares of construction paper to fit the graph squares

- glue sticks

Activity

Write "Favorite Sandwich Graph" across the top of the paper or poster board. Write the names of the sandwiches you have talked about at intervals across the bottom of the graph. Add names of other sandwiches students suggest, such as tuna or egg salad. Give students squares of construction paper and ask them to affix their squares of paper to the graph, creating vertical columns above the sandwich names. (See Week 34, Day 3, for an example.)

Background

The United Nations was founded on October 24, 1945. Its first meetings were in San Francisco, and delegates went there from all over the world after World War II to begin this exciting project. The United Nations now has its headquarters in New York City.

Making It Work

This is a great time to promote understanding of cultural diversity by learning a little bit about children and customs around the world. You can base your week's social studies curriculum on a number of age-appropriate books that children will enjoy and perhaps try to read on their own.

Day 1—Bread Around the World

Materials

- *Bread Bread Bread* by Ann Morris (Lothrop, Lee & Shepard, 1989)
- classroom wall map of the world
- globe

Activity

Bread Bread Bread is a great follow-up to the sandwich unit in Week 42. It discusses bread around the world with beautiful photographs and minimal text. The appendix provides enough basic facts about each picture to serve as a primer for the study of world cultures.

Read this book aloud to your students and encourage class discussion.

Help students find each of the places mentioned in the book on the world map and/or globe.

List the names of the countries you locate on the board and leave them there for the remainder of the week. Students can go back and find the places again on the map or globe during their free time.

Day 2—Rice from Around the World

Materials

- *Everybody Cooks Rice* by Norah Dooley (Carolrhoda Books, 1991)
- classroom wall map of the world
- globe

Activity

This book continues the international food theme in a story that takes place in the United States. A girl looks for her brother and in the process is invited to sample rice dishes being prepared in the homes of their multicultural neighborhood. Recipes for the dishes are included at the end of the book. Students might want to copy them or check out the book to try one or more recipes at home.

Read this book aloud to your students and encourage class discussion.

Help students find each of the places mentioned in the book on the world map and/or globe.

List the names of the countries you locate on the board and leave them there for the remainder of the week. Students can go back and find them again on the map or globe during their free time.

You could also make a chart like the one below and help students complete it.

Rice Around the World	
Country	**Rice Dish**

Day 3—Games Around the World

Materials

- *Games of the World: How to Make Them, How to Play Them, How They Came to Be*, special English edition for the National Committees for UNICEF in Australia, Canada, Ireland, and Switzerland. (Frederic V. Grunfeld, Swiss Committee for UNICEF, 1982)
- classroom wall map of the world
- globe

Activity

Pick a playground game from the book, teach it to your class, and play it at P.E. or recess during the week to celebrate United Nations Day.

Day 4—Hopscotch Around the World

Materials

- *Hopscotch Around the World* by Mary D. Lankford (Morrow, 1992)
- classroom wall map of the world
- globe

Activity

Read this book aloud to your students and find the countries in which the nineteen variations of hopscotch originated on the map and/or globe.

Let students decide on one or more of the games they would like to try.

Use sidewalk chalk on the playground blacktop to draw the diagrams found in the text.

Day 5—Breakfast Around the World

Materials

- *Is Anybody Up?* Ellen Kandoian (Putnam's, 1989)
- classroom wall map of the world
- globe

Activity

This book also traces food from different cultures, but only within the eastern time zone. A short essay following the main text helps teachers with introducing the concept of time zones.

Read this book aloud to your students and encourage class discussion.

Help students find each of the places mentioned in the book on the world map and/or globe.

List the names of the countries you locate on the board and leave them there for the following week or so. Students can go back and find them again on the map or globe during their free time.

Background

Two thousand years ago, October 31 marked the Celtic New Year's Eve in Britain and Northern Europe. The Celts feasted on that night and told stories about their ancestors. They believed that the spirits of people who had died during the year wandered about that night, cold, hungry, and angry that the living were able to stay inside, warm and full. So when the Celts went outside on that night, they carried lanterns and wore disguises to keep from being recognized by the spirits. They also left gifts of food and drink on the doorsteps for them.

When church leaders tried to convert the Celts to Christianity, they simply added their religious beliefs to the Celtic ones. They made November first All Saints' Day and November second All Souls' Day, respectively, both of which honor the spirits of the dead. October 31 became the Eve of All Saints, or All Hallows' Eve. All Hallows' Eve eventually became known as Halloween.

The customs of the Celts came to the United States with the people who migrated here from Britain and Northern Europe. Although some customs have changed, we still carry lanterns, wear scary disguises, and present gifts of food to one another on Halloween.

Making It Work

Although you may be interested in the background information, students will naturally be more concerned with the fun of Halloween—telling spooky stories, making jack-o'-lanterns, and wearing costumes.

Day 1—What Are You Going to Be?

Materials

- writing materials
- crayons

Activity

Have students write (or dictate to you or to an instructional assistant) a description of what they plan to be for Halloween. Ask them to tell why they chose a particular costume.

When students finish, help them edit and copy their stories. They can then illustrate and display the stories on your seasonal bulletin board.

Day 2—Safe and Sane Jack-o'-Lanterns

Materials

- several large pumpkins or small individual squashes
- scratch paper and pencils
- markers
- poster paint or tempera
- paint brushes

Activity

Have children create jack-o'-lanterns from uncarved pumpkins by painting faces on them.

You can divide the class into groups to work cooperatively on large pumpkins or give each student a small individual squash.

Ask students to plan their face designs on paper first and then to sketch them on the pumpkins or squashes with markers before painting so that the finished projects will appear the way they wish them to look.

Display large jack-o'-lanterns around the room. Display individual squashes on the desks of their creators.

Day 3—Tissue Ghosts

Materials

- large box of white tissues
- black and white thread
- fine-line black markers

Activity

Help students make quick and easy floating ghosts. For each ghost, crumple one tissue into a ball. Lay the ball of tissue in the center of another tissue and gather the second tissue around the ball to create a head. Tie with white thread. Draw eyes and mouth with black marker, taking care because the ink tends to run. Suspend ghosts from the ceiling with lengths of black thread.

Day 4—Paper Bag Masks

Materials

- one large paper grocery bag for each student
- markers
- construction paper
- scissors
- glue sticks
- assorted art supplies

Activity

Help each student find the right place to cut eyes in his or her paper bag for seeing.

Let students design their own paper bag masks to create any characters they wish. Some easy ones are robots, birds, and monsters.

Put them aside to wear for a Halloween party on Friday.

Day 5—It's Party Time

Materials

- party supplies
- party food (jack-o'-lantern cupcakes or cookies and orange punch)
- apples for games
- a book of spooky stories

Activity

End the day and the week with a party.

Students can wear their paper bag masks until it is time to eat or pin the masks around the room as decorations.

Play some games. The apple games listed in Week 37, Day 5, would be appropriate.

Finish up with a story.

Take down the ghosts, masks, and stories and send them home with your students.

Day 2—Disneyland or Disney World?

Materials

- printed materials such as travel brochures showing the attractions at both Disneyland in California and Disney World in Florida
- encyclopedias or other illustrated reference materials

Activity

Find out from your students if any of them have visited a Disney theme park.

Pass out brochures and give everyone enough time to look at and compare the features of both parks.

Have students write (or dictate to you or an instructional assistant) about their choice of these subjects:

- why they liked the theme park they went to, if they have been to one
- which theme park they would like to visit, if they had the chance

When students have finished, have them share and discuss their ideas.

Day 3—Mouse Ears

Materials

- plain plastic headbands
- black construction paper
- circle patterns
- scissors, tape

Activity

Have each student trace two circles on black construction paper and cut them out. Attach the circles to the headbands with tape. Students can then wear and enjoy their mouse ears.

Day 4—List And Choose

Materials

- writing materials

Activity

Ask students to tell you which Disney videos they have at home.

List the titles on the chalkboard as they are given.

Have students discuss the various choices listed.

Explain secret ballots: Don't show anyone your vote. Don't sign your name.

Give students paper and have them vote for the video they would like to see.

Count the ballots and announce the winner and the runner-up (in case of film failure or forgetfulness).

Send notes home with the students who own the videos, asking to borrow them for Day 5.

Day 5—Disney Film Festival

Materials

- video voted as favorite on Day 4
- mouse ears

Activity

Put on your mouse ears and enjoy the film. When it is over ask students:

   Did you enjoy it?

   What part(s) did you like best? Why?

Finish off the week by teaching your students the words to the Mickey Mouse theme song or by singing "Happy Birthday" to Mickey Mouse.

Background

December 13 is the Swedish feast honoring St. Lucia. Santa Lucia is a Sicilian saint; no one knows how she came to be such an important figure in Sweden. "Lucia" does, however, mean "light," and the celebration reminds people that the long dark nights of winter will soon grow shorter.

Making It Work

Plan a St. Lucia Day party and invite the parents of your students. Make and send home the invitations on the first day so they can arrange their time in order to attend.

Day 1—Invitations

Materials

- white drawing paper
- markers
- gold star stickers

Activity

Have each student make an invitation for his or her parents. Decorate the front of the card with gold stars. Complete the invitation below and attach it to the inside of the card.

You are cordially invited to our

St. Lucia Day Party

_____
Date

_____
Time

_____
Place

R.S.V.P.

Day 2—St. Lucia Facts

Materials

- encyclopedias or other illustrated reference materials
- classroom wall map of the world

Activity

This is designed to be an oral exercise to establish a general base of information. See what the students already know and give them the information they don't have. Expand on and discuss the different ideas for reinforcement.

- December 13 is the Swedish feast of St. Lucia.

- It honors Santa Lucia of Sicily and no one knows how it came to be such an important day in Sweden.

- "Lucia" means "light" and the celebration reminds people that the long dark nights of winter will soon grow shorter.

- The children of the family put on the ceremony for their parents, waking them with coffee and saffron buns early on the morning of St. Lucia Day.

- The oldest daughter plays the part of St. Lucia. She wears a long white dress with a red sash and a crown of lighted candles in her hair.

- Her sisters, also dressed in white, follow in a procession, carrying candles. Her brothers wear long white shirts painted with gold stars.

- In Sweden, people have St. Lucia processions not only at home but also in schools, churches, and offices.

Day 3—St. Lucia Crowns

Materials

- construction paper
- scissors
- glue
- stapler

Activity

Make crowns for the girls in the class. Make a headband from construction paper. Staple the ends together. Cover with flowers cut from construction paper. Cut out five paper candles for each girl. Glue them to the headband so the candles stand straight. (See page 149.)

Day 4—Star Boy Hats

Materials

- construction paper
- scissors
- gold stars
- stapler
- glue

Activity

Make star boy hats for the boys. Roll white construction paper into a cone shape to fit each boy's head. Staple. Decorate with gold stars. (See below.)

Day 5—St. Lucia Party

Materials

- party supplies (white and gold, if possible)
- Swedish cookies and punch

Activity

Have students form a procession and serve refreshments to their parents. After the refreshments have been eaten, the students can tell their parents some of the facts they have learned about this holiday.

Background

The winter solstice, which occurs on December 21 or 22, is the shortest day of the year in the northern hemisphere. The farther north one goes, the fewer the hours of daylight. If you go far enough north, there will be days when there is no sunlight at all. The winter solstice occurs six months after the summer solstice, which is the longest day of the year. (These events are reversed in the southern hemisphere.)

Making It Work

Have students look at this event from the point of view of primitive people who had no idea why the days grew shorter and, at least in the far north, the sun disappeared.

Day 1—Scientific Facts

Materials

- encyclopedia or other illustrated reference materials
- classroom wall map of the world
- globe

Activity

This is designed to be an oral exercise to establish a general base of information. See what the students already know and give them the information they don't have. Expand on and discuss the different ideas for reinforcement.

- The winter solstice, which occurs on December 21 or 22, is the shortest day of the year in the northern hemisphere.

- The farther north one goes, the fewer the hours of daylight.

- If you go far enough north, there will be times when there is no sunlight at all.

- The winter solstice occurs six months after the summer solstice, which is the longest day of the year.

- These events are reversed in the southern hemisphere.

Day 2—Scientific Facts Demonstration

Materials

- globe
- lamp or flashlight

Activity

Demonstrate how the tilting of the earth on its axis causes the days to grow shorter in winter in the northern hemisphere.

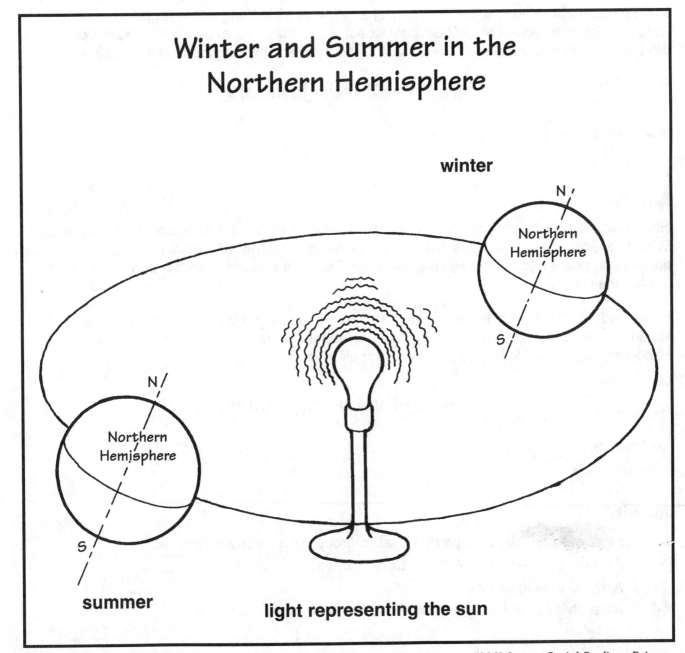

Winter and Summer in the Northern Hemisphere

Day 3—Myth Making

Materials

• writing materials

Activity

Remind students that myths are a kind of folklore that explains nature for people who do not have science. Ancient people did not know why the days were getting shorter in the winter. They were afraid when the sun did not rise at all. They made up myths to explain what was happening.

Have students pretend that they are part of a primitive tribe living in the far north. Ask them to write (or dictate to you or an instructional assistant) a story that explains what is happening to the sun. When everyone is finished, have students share their myths and discuss them.

Day 4—Creating Rituals

Materials

• writing materials

Activity

Have students divide into cooperative groups. Each group will be a separate primitive tribe living in the far north. The days are getting shorter and shorter and colder again, and the sun finally disappears altogether. Have each group design a ritual to save the sun and make it strong again.

Have students discuss, plan, and write down the rituals they design. Give help as needed. When everyone is ready, have each group perform its ritual for the rest of the class. Encourage students to discuss and explain their ideas.

Day 5—Evaluating Rituals

Materials

• none

Activity

Use the following questions to prompt a large-group discussion about ritual.

Did primitive people think their rituals worked?

Why did they think so?

What always happened after they performed their rituals?

Background

Christmas, December 25, celebrates the birth of Jesus Christ. Many Christians begin their celebration on December 24, Christmas Eve. It was on Christmas Eve that Mary and Joseph found refuge in a stable in Bethlehem, and angels were said to have appeared to shepherds tending their flocks outside the city to announce the birth of the Christ Child.

Making It Work

Many symbols are associated with Christmas: stars, holly, trees, angels, and so on. Perhaps the most important symbol of Christmas is the "gift giver." Many different countries and cultures have their own gift givers.

Day 1—Santa Claus

Materials

- encyclopedias or other illustrated reference materials

Activity

This is designed to be an oral exercise to establish a general base of information. See what the students already know and give them the information they don't have. Expand on and discuss the different ideas for reinforcement.

- Santa Claus is the gift giver we have in the United States.

- He is the gift giver in other parts of the world, too, where he is sometimes known as St. Nicholas.

- He has not always looked the way he does today. Over the years, his facial appearance as well as his clothing have changed.

- In some countries he comes on a sled pulled by reindeer, as he does in the United States, but in other countries he walks or rides a horse. In Australia, he arrives on a surf board.

- In the United States many children leave cookies and milk or some other snack for Santa. In some countries children leave a snack of straw or oats for the reindeer.

Day 2—Other Gift Givers

Materials

- encyclopedias or other illustrated reference materials

Activity

Depending on the age group you are teaching, help students find information about these gift givers or have them use research materials on their own.

Name _____   Date _____

Gift Givers Around The World	
Gift Giver	**Country**
Grandpa Koleda	
Julemanden	
Juletompte	
Grandmother Babushka	
Befana	
Kristkind	
Father Christmas	
Le Pere Noël	
Papa Noel	
Sinterklaas	

Day 3—The Christmas Tree

Materials

- *The Night Tree* by Eve Bunting (Harcourt Brace Jovanovich, 1991)

Activity

Tell your students that there are many stories about the Christmas tree. This is a modern story about one family's Christmas tree tradition.

Read *The Night Tree* (32 pages) aloud to your class.

Day 4—A Magic Journey

Materials

- *The Polar Express* by Chris Van Allsburg (Houghton & Mifflin, 1985)
- tiny jingle bells for each student (if desired)

Activity

This is a wonderful books with beautiful illustrations.

Read *The Polar Express* (32 pages) aloud to your class.

Day 5—Another Magic Journey

Materials

- video version of *The Snowman* by Raymond Briggs, based on his book of the same name

Activity

This film was an Academy Award nominee. The original music, composed and conducted by Howard Blake, is also outstanding.

Show *The Snowman* to your class to finish up the week.

Background

Kwanzaa is celebrated for seven days from December 26 through January 1. It is a cultural holiday designed to recognize the cultural heritage shared by Americans of African descent. It was originated by Dr. Maulana Karenga, chairman of the black studies department at California State University, Long Beach. Although it was not intended as a substitute for Christmas and New Year's, it can be used either in this way or as an addition to the more traditional holidays.

Making It Work

Kwanzaa embodies some deep principles that may be too abstract for children in the primary grades. There are parts of the celebration, however, that they will enjoy learning about and participating in.

Day 1—Symbols

Materials

- examples of each of the symbols (Children might be able to bring them from home.)

- *Kwanzaa: Everything You Always Wanted to Know but Didn't Know Where to Ask* by Cedric McClester, Gumbs & Thomas, 1990

Activity

This is designed to be an oral exercise to establish a general base of information. See what the students already know and give them the information they don't have. Expand on and discuss the different ideas for reinforcement.

The seven basic symbols of Kwanzaa are:

- Fruits and vegetables

- Placemat (mkeka)

- Candleholder (kinara)

- Candles (one black, three red, three green)

- Ears of corn

- Gifts

- Special holiday cup

Day 2—Making a Kinara

Materials

- _Kwanzaa: Everything You Always Wanted to Know but Didn't Know Where to Ask_ by Cedric McClester (Gumbs & Thomas, 1990)
- a piece of wood and seven long tacks for each student
- strong glue

Activity

The kinara or candle holder for Kwanzaa can be very simple.

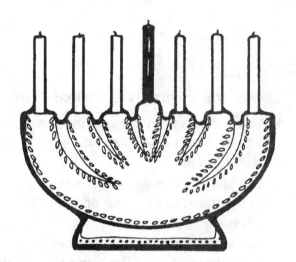

1. Sand the piece of wood, which can be painted or left unfinished.
2. Glue on the tacks, with the points sticking up, at even intervals. Let dry completely.
3. Simply stick a candle down on each tack.

Day 3—Making Kwanzaa Cards

Materials

- _Kwanzaa: Everything You Always Wanted to Know but Didn't Know Where to Ask_ by Cedric McClester (Gumbs & Thomas, 1990)

Materials

- black, red, and green construction paper (Kwanzaa colors)
- scissors
- glue sticks
- markers

Activity

Have students make Kwanzaa cards for their families. The seven principles of Kwanzaa can be written on the front of the card and a personal message written inside. Use red or green for the basic card so the writing will show. Decorate with black and the remaining color.

The principles are

- Unity
- Self-determination
- Collective work and responsibility
- Cooperative economics
- Purpose
- Creativity
- Faith

Day 4—Making a Mkeka

Materials

- *Kwanzaa: Everything You Always Wanted to Know but Didn't Know Where to Ask* by Cedric McCluster (Gumbs & Thomas, 1990)
- black, red, and green construction paper (Kwanzaa colors)
- scissors
- tape

Activity

A mkeka, or placemat, is fun to make. An easy way to do it is by weaving paper.

1. Measure and draw lines the long way at one-half inch (1.25 cm) intervals on one sheet of paper.
2. Cut along the lines, stopping one inch (2.5 cm) away from the edges of the paper.
3. Cut lengthwise strips about one inch (2.5 cm) wide from the other two strips of paper.
4. Weave the strips in and out of the slits in the first piece of paper, alternating colors.
5. Fold the ends of the strips over and tape down on the back.

Day 5—The Kwanzaa Feast

Materials

- *Kwanzaa: Everything You Always Wanted to Know but Didn't Know Where to Ask* by Cedric McCluster (Gumbs & Thomas, 1990)
- plates and utensils
- placemats
- Kwanzaa food (See below.)

Activity

The food for the Kwanzaa Karumu (feast) is very elaborate for school, consisting of chicken, fish, rice, yams, and so on, all prepared in authentic African styles. If a parent or group of parents wants to provide a Kwanzaa feast, you may welcome the effort, but you can still be true to the spirit of Kwanzaa simply by serving a selection of cut–up raw vegetables and dips.

Index

Index